THE SUFFICIENCY OF GOD

Not that we are sufficient of ourselves
to think anything as of ourselves;
but our sufficiency is of God.
II CORINTHIANS 3.5

★

Pierre Maury, Karl Barth, W. A. Visser 't Hooft in 1934

Archbishop Nikodim welcomed by Dr Ernest Payne and Dr Visser 't Hooft to World Council of Churches, New Delhi 1961

THE SUFFICIENCY
OF GOD

★

*Essays on the Ecumenical Hope
in Honor of W. A. Visser 't Hooft*

★

EDITED BY
ROBERT C. MACKIE
AND
CHARLES C. WEST

The Westminster Press
PHILADELPHIA

PRINTED IN GREAT BRITAIN
Published by The Westminster Press_R
Philadelphia 7, Pennsylvania

CONTENTS

* Translated by Charles C. West

W. A. VISSER 'T HOOFT:
AN APPRECIATION

Robert C. Mackie

WHEN the Faith and Order and the Life and Work Movements laid plans in 1937 for the creation of the World Council of Churches it was an act of faith which saw beyond actual affinities of outlook. Many delegates went on from the Oxford Conference on 'Church Community and State' to the Edinburgh Conference on Faith and Order. But they were conscious of two different areas of concern. 'Edinburgh' had its attention fixed on the Church; 'Oxford' was troubled about the world. Certainly the two movements were seen to belong together, but how were natural preoccupations and prejudices to be overcome?

The two movements discovered that they had one asset in common: a prospective General Secretary. To W. A. Visser 't Hooft they turned with unanimous enthusiasm. He had been active in both of them. With Dr J. H. Oldham he had pioneered in the social and political thinking for the Oxford Conference; he was also deeply involved in the doctrinal and liturgical discussions of the churches. But it was not only his experience and competence in the two organizations which made this Dutchman, still in his thirties, the inevitable choice for the key post in a difficult new venture; it was his unusually flexible mind. There was in him a zest for life in its wholeness which was ideal for ecumenical service.

The turbulence of the ten years which followed the first meeting of the Provisional Committee of the World Council of Churches in 1938 might well have wrecked the fragile framework. In fact they strengthened it. But it was due in large measure to the General Secretary's sensitiveness and persistence that the 'process of formation' was completed in time for the founding Assembly of Amsterdam 1948. Certainly his experience in the World's Student Christian Federation stood him in good stead, giving him personal contacts and the knowledge of how to take initiative. But it was his ability to use his experience, and to draw the different elements of the ecumenical movement together so that a coherent unity of purpose began to emerge, that was his special gift, and it has never deserted him. Now Evanston 1954 and New Delhi 1961 have in their turn become ecumenical milestones. The integration of the International Missionary Council and the World Council has been accomplished. The new headquarters in Geneva is nearing completion. And it becomes difficult to imagine how the world relationships of the churches could have taken any other course. So, before history hardens into the inevitable, we should pause in 1963 and realize that this amazing quarter of a century of developing understanding between the churches constitutes one man's semi-jubilee of service.

One of the difficulties in assessing W. A. Visser 't Hooft's contribution as General Secretary of the World Council is that there is no comparable position in the life of the churches. There is a sense in which the World Council stands apart from the member churches with its own intellectual and moral authority. Its General Secretary represents a wider consensus of Christian opinion and initiative than any confessional church leader. There is also a sense in which the World Council—in its determined rejection of the idea of a super-church—is powerless without the goodwill and executive action of the member churches. Its General Secretary is the servant who must always be verifying his mandate. For him to have an assured, unassailable position would involve drastic and crippling limits to his usefulness. The remarkable thing about W. A. Visser 't Hooft is that he has established the office without having to try to magnify its importance. How has he done this?

The first requirement, of course, was simply to begin at the beginning. He has played a formative part in creating all the organs and practices of the Council. His imprint is on its administration. Some people perhaps regret that, because it has not always worked out well in details. But ecumenical relationships are notoriously difficult to streamline. And for Visser 't Hooft the main concern has always been that the right ideas and relationships should not be kept from fruition by too great concentration on procedures. This whole issue can be argued to and fro according to personal or national temperament. Complaints are inevitably vocal at large meetings such as the New Delhi Assembly, or whenever a cherished project miscarries. What cannot be gainsaid is that a remarkable output of common thought and action has been made possible.

One of the most striking illustrations of W. A. Visser 't Hooft's gifts can be seen in the way in which the original 'movements' developed into a formal Council. In its initial stages the ecumenical enterprise was carried forward by people who had grown up in it, who had the particular vision and enthusiasm of amateurs. From Amsterdam the constitution laid greater weight upon the official action of churches, and brought, in many cases, a different group of responsible church leaders on to its committees. The first Central Committee was considerably different in professional texture from the composition of committees which had preceded it. The official creation of the Council might have killed the spontaneity of the years of its formation. It was in no small measure due to the

General Secretary's genius for stimulating interest and conviction in those he works with that enabled such a vital and
creative transition to be carried through.

I referred earlier to W. A. Visser 't Hooft's familiarity with
the work of both Life and Work and Faith and Order. This
was not due simply to the freedom of passage in ecumenical
circles which his leadership in the World's Student Christian
Federation had given him. It was due to the breadth of his
intellectual interest. Fascinated by theology he was deeply
concerned with the integrity of the life of the churches. He
had no interest in ecclesiastical short-cuts or in extra-
ecclesiastical Christianity. His patience could never be
exhausted if there was a real problem to be considered. He had
no intolerance for sincerely held opinions which countered
his own. On the other hand he was no academic theologian.
The world also fascinated him and the problems it presented
must always be faced on their merits. The Church must never
assume that it had all the answers. Christian theology must
learn to be serviceable. Its stand must never be theoretical; it
must have a bearing upon the immediate human dilemmas.
To sum up, the new General Secretary was not primarily an
administrator, nor primarily a theologian, nor primarily a man
of the world. He was a Christian with a lively mind who was
prepared to do the hard work necessary for the realization of
some of his dreams.

One or two memories of the pioneering years may help at
this stage to get the picture into focus. There is that lovely
autumn day in 1938 when I stepped out of my first plane to
Geneva and was greeted with a shout from 'Wim'. (For so I
must now call him since this appreciation is of a man and not
of a public figure!) He was sitting at a table in the open air at
what was then a very rustic airfield. Our meeting was to
consider the effects of the Munich Crisis and Settlement upon
our international Christian concerns. It was a strange moment
for a General Secretary to take on a largely undefined

responsibility, but Wim showed at once that calculated determination to go right ahead with anything that could be done, which was to stand the World Council in such good stead during the years of war.

I think next of a visit to the old Champel headquarters of the WCC on the day that Holland was over-run. How to comfort a man who had been bereaved of his country? We talked quietly about what might lie ahead for him. But he at once showed that sense of knowing where he had been put by God and willingness to stay there, which meant that he would never desert his post. And as it happened he did not desert his country either, but performed most signal services for it, just because he was stationed in Geneva.

All through the war years Wim's letters came to me in Canada from Geneva, frequently by several routes. Often they contained articles or reflections or reports which could be put to instant use in North America and Britain. To be in contact with the European Resistance on the one hand, and with the wider planning of the outside world on the other, stimulated Wim into a creativity of ideas which gave shape to men's aspirations far beyond his personal contacts. And so when we suddenly and unexpectedly met again in a London restaurant in the early winter of 1944, I found him with his customary grasp of the world situation. He had flown with doubtful legality from Brussels, having got that length by means best known to him; but here he was, not lingering in the grim past or absorbed in the exciting present, but raising the relevant issues for the future and looking out, as always, for new colleagues.

When the war ended there were all the plans to be made for that meeting without precedent—the First Assembly at Amsterdam. And now after Amsterdam came the regular sequence of Central Committee meetings and conferences in which Wim was to be by no means the most prominent, but always the most indispensable, figure. My clearest impression of the man himself, even in the post-war years, are of snatched occasions in cafés, of leisurely evenings of talk in his home or mine, of intermittent comments on journeys when Wim was feeling his way ahead for the right idea, the right man, the right occasion. For example there was the bitter winter morning when we took the local train to Celigny, climbed into a gig and jogged up the long avenue to the Château de Bossey, stood with our hats on and muffled up in the perishing cold of the salons with their empire furniture and Napoleonic miniatures, and decided that this was the place for the Ecumenical Institute! And of course the Institute was entirely the product of Wim's far-seeing intelligence. A world movement that did not think, and prepare men and women to think, held no interest for him.

Often in the following years when Wim drove me back in his car from a visit to the Institute, I realized how strongly his personal inclination would have led him to teach rather than to direct affairs. Indeed his room in the headquarters 'chalet', with the great old-fashioned desk in front of him covered with untidy heaps of papers and odd mementos, has always looked more like a scholar's den than an executive's office. The grind of correspondence, documents and committees has never quelled the impatience with accepted forms, the directness of thought and frankness of speech which have endeared him to several generations of students, and make him such an acceptable speaker to laymen and youth today.

Whether later General Secretaries of the World Council should be theologians is a nice question! But we can be thankful that its first has been a man to whom biblical and theological studies are meat and drink. Wim has always enthusiastically revered Karl Barth, and that might superficially appear a disadvantage in the kaleidoscopic theological background of a Council of Churches. Dogmatism of all things would seem to be out of place. Yet just that dogmatism has saved so many ecumenical discussions from banality. And to those who themselves were strong in their convictions it has never given offence. For Wim's dogmatism springs from humility. It is the insistence of a man, who has no desire to dismiss lightly other men's knowledge of God, that God himself must come first.

Indeed this spontaneous enthusiasm for biblical reality is the key to Wim's personality. General discussions about strategy and responsibilities have always bored him, and he is not good at concealing the fact! But give the matter in hand an immediate practical turn, bring it into the realm of here and now for an individual, for a committee or for the Council and Wim is all attention. When a document that someone else was to write does not appear in time, Wim writes it. When a discussion looks like foundering, Wim is undismayed and with some shrewd comments keeps it moving to a useful conclusion. When the wind of opinion veers against ecumenical progress, and the ship seems to be losing way, Wim holds it steadily on its course as if nothing adverse was happening. No route is too long or too tedious, no business too mundane or too trivial, if thereby the essential truth of God's Sovereignty can be seen.

Wim's knowledge of what has happened and is happening within the ecumenical orbit is encyclopaedic. But what has made him the outstanding ecumenical leader is his gift of selection and focus. His reports to the Central Committees and to the Assemblies of the World Council have never been dramatic personal *tours d'horizon*. They have always picked out one or two points which were relevant at that precise moment, which are seen at once to be key points, and which no other mind could have selected with such perceptive precision. And then they are stated, with no rhetorical tricks which would give them a personal identification, but in exceptionally lucid summary which puts them in the category of things you cannot forget because you are persuaded that you might have thought of them yourself! This is a great art, not to pose as an intellectual giant who pioneers men's thinking, but to take your crowd with you on the basis of what they already know, or might have been supposed to know, conveying an illumination which was previously lacking.

His gift of creating and registering advance in ecumenical thought and action has sometimes provoked the suspicion that Wim is Machiavellian in his use of power! Certainly he has not set out to dominate the World Council machine administratively. He has always had a considerable distaste for detailed administration. Eager to let others take responsibility, he has retained in his hands, not so much the reins of power, as the impulses of growth and direction. Indeed his colleagues have sometimes expressed embarrassment or even indignation because of lack of administrative action, of allowing situations to drift. Seldom has any objection been made to General Secretarial interference! Perhaps indeed the difficulty has been to see what he sees and therefore to understand how at the centre he is really holding the whole show together. The shrewdest criticism has been of his intransigence, rather than of his dominance! But that genuine trait in his character springs from a total conviction about the existence and function of the World Council which is unsurpassed, and perhaps unrivalled.

Now surely this is a very great debt we owe to Wim. To be concerned solely with the thing itself and never with its administrative proportions, or accessory functions, is the peculiar gift of the devotee. Wim has never desired the World Council to do this or that, except in so far as doing was being. He has been concerned with the root idea of unity, with—to use his own phrase—'the Pressure of our Common Calling'. He has been concerned with manifestations of unity only in so far as they genuinely serve the calling of the People of God. That is why the WCC has developed, not merely into a great organization which it almost accidentally has become, but into an accepted fact of the life of the churches, a reminder that the Spirit still speaks to them, an historic embodiment of the idea of the wholeness of the Church in the thinking of confessional or national units.

Now all this could be dangerous. It might be the creation of a structure for men's thinking which later they would regret, if it were not very simply defined by its relation to the Will of God. *'Dieu le veut'* is a favourite quotation of Visser 't Hooft. He used it at New Delhi. The ecumenical movement is for him, quite simply, an expression of what God would have the churches be and do. It is a matter of obedience, and obedience is not a question of blue-prints but going where you are told to go. And so Wim is never deflected. He may change his mind; he is very susceptible to new ideas, and moves with great rapidity along a fresh direction; but the thread of following the divine purpose remains unchanged.

It is Wim's single-mindedness which makes personal relations with him an exhilarating and, let it be admitted, sometimes a devastating experience! It would be false to conceal that he does not suffer fools gladly. The trouble is that he does not notice them—to their chagrin! Any carefully planned approach to the General Secretary, or self-conscious assumption of importance, will always be a total loss because Wim will not waste time in preliminaries. But any sincere query or real human problem will always meet with a quick response. Too quick sometimes? A mind that sweeps aside the irrelevant and instantly reaches for essentials may sometimes be in error, but not for long. Stopped in his tracks by objection or protest he will think again without rancour. Indeed the absence of pique, the inability to take personal offence, is awkwardly disarming! You can have a disagreement, even a sharp disagreement, with Wim, but you cannot basically quarrel with him. The sufficient reason for Wim is that a quarrel would delay the discovery of truth, and truth is all. A World Council of Churches cannot afford to have parties because it is concerned with God and the discovery of his will is primary.

But this sounds inhuman, and Wim is very human. From time to time he gets mad at his old friends because they do not see the new situation he sees, but he will never lose affection and respect for them. Anyone else who starts to run them down will receive a sharp rejoinder. It has often been a joy to see Wim with a group of colleagues or fellow members of Committee on a 'day off' in the middle of a meeting, or at that glorious moment when all is done that can be done and there are yet a few hours to spare. Then—to the astonishment of newer acquaintances—a rather 'puckish' Wim emerges, bent on some exploit or expedition or celebration which is wholly irrelevant and therefore just right for the occasion. It is in these 'off-guard' moments, when all controversy and preoccupation are dismissed, that many a church leader has had his loyalty to the ecumenical movement most unusually confirmed.

How can one say more without a breach of confidence? There must be hundreds of men and women who are proud that they have Wim's friendship, who feel it gives a mark of significance to lives which they know lack so many of the notes that his possesses. The striking thing is the variety of these men and women. They belong to all the generations of the writers in this volume; they are of many races and confessions; they are by no means all 'egg-heads' or 'high-brows'; their conversation has been carried on in four different languages; they are not all church-leaders or even churchmen; their contacts with him have been of many different kinds at many levels. But all would acknowledge a sense of exhilaration from his zest for life, and a centrality of Christian purpose to which his companionship has always stimulated them. That is the basic reason for the character of this volume. Tributes to the man himself would have tended to hide the axiom by which he has always lived, that our sufficiency is of God.

BIBLICAL THEOLOGY IN THE ECUMENICAL STRUGGLE

Josef L. Hromadka

I T is impossible to write on this subject without direct reference to W. A. Visser 't Hooft, for whom I have a deep affection, and whose ecumenical leadership I never cease to appreciate. I do not know anyone who would be better fitted for the position he now occupies in the ecumenical movement, not only organizationally, but also personally and morally. Over and over again I have tried to discover the very roots of his authority and strength. After twenty years, and even more, of his activity as the leading secretary of the ecumenical movement, his influence and personal prestige have in no way diminished. On the contrary, many of us wonder who might, in foreseeable time, adequately replace him and continue his work. But it is not our business to meditate on this matter. The Lord of our life and death, present in our midst as Jesus of Nazareth, knows better than we do how to guide the minds and hearts of those who will be responsible for the selection of new men.

The days when Wim Visser 't Hooft and I met first and got to know one another are, historically speaking, far away. It was at the General Committee of the World's Student Christian Federation at Nyborg, in Denmark, in 1926. John R. Mott was then an unrivalled leader of the Student Christian

Movement, and a great missionary statesman. The catastrophe of the First World War was being gradually forgotten, and the aspirations and hopes of Western Christianity were persuasively interpreted by this great man. The perspective of 'The Evangelization of the World in this Generation' may have already passed its zenith, but it was still maintained by a group of devoted missionaries and young Christian students. We did not fully realize the depth of the crisis in which the post-war world found itself. I had a feeling, and I believe Visser 't Hooft shared it with me, that Western Christian churches were undergoing a period of theological and spiritual malady, and that the Student Movement was weakened by the lack of a burning faith and of a sense of destiny. Western Christianity and Western democracy, to which I and my countrymen adhered, had been undermined in a most disastrous way. But we were not fully aware of this situation; we were only disturbed by the growing atmosphere of a sceptical and relativist mood permeating the life of our nations, and consequently of students also. Nevertheless the vision of the evangelization of the world was still alive, and John R. Mott's leadership unquestioned. He was a link between the beginning of the ecumenical movement in 1910 and the post-war era.

Exactly in those days and years, in the middle of the 'twenties, the creative and dynamic force of the theology of crisis became evident. It was still in the margin of contemporary theology, and ecumenical activity. Neither 'Stockholm' nor 'Lausanne' were affected by the new theology. The younger generation, however, to which Visser 't Hooft belonged, not only took notice of the theological revival passing through European theological schools, but also realized the essential need to overcome the disintegrating consequences of liberalism, and to lay better and solider foundations for the work of churches, missionary movements, student groups, and, of course, the ecumenical movement. Looking back at that period of our activity both in the SCM and in ecumenical projects, I see today even more clearly than before the providential character of dialectical theology, or whatever we may call it, for undergirding the manifold responsibilities placed on the shoulders of Christian Churches and their leaders. The secret of Visser 't Hooft's powerful leadership may rest exactly on this very fact. He never gave up the vision heralded by John R. Mott, the vision of a great Christian statesman, who was aware of the mission of the Church in the modern world; but Visser 't Hooft was also aware of the malady of the modern mind affecting both theology and the Church in all its manifestations, and of the indispensable rethinking and revival of the substance of the Gospel and the Church.

Visser 't Hooft was armed against the easy optimism of the modern Christian mind, which was prevalent in those days in the Anglo-Saxon, primarily the American world, and at the same time against the dangers of an abstract, self-sufficient, self-righteous academic theology, unrelated to the filth and dust of ordinary life. I still recall with what interest I read his book *The Background of the Social Gospel in America*, published in 1928. It was providential that he devoted so much of his youthful energy to the study of American theology and of its most characteristic expression in the Social Gospel. He penetrated into the background of American Christian activism and pragmatism with all its creative aspects. He did it without any mood of European theological superiority or proud superciliousness. But he did it with a desire to help the practical mind of American Christians by relating it to the very source of the biblical, prophetic and apostolic message. The great achievements and potentialities of American Christianity must not be wasted by shallow liberalism and by a careless equation of the Gospel with the American understanding of man and democracy—with 'the American way of life'.

It has been most fortunate that a genuine European theologian, who had gone through a vital theological revival, while retaining a deep appreciation of Anglo-Saxon and

American Christianity, should be selected as the leading organizer of the World Council of Churches. Furthermore, this very continental theologian by his national origin and practical experience with youth and students from all over the world has had an open mind for the almost abysmal changes going on in the non-Western and non-Christian world. World War II revealed to him the historical character of the world revolution and liberated him from many of the inhibitions and fears of the average Western man, who was unable to transcend his inherited political, cultural and social criteria, and who felt terribly frustrated under the impact of what was happening after 1945.

Looking at Visser 't Hooft and watching the way he has acted as one of the most important ecumenical leaders, I have realized how much a really vital biblical theology means for the ecumenical struggle. The deeper we dig into the hidden sources of the Prophets, of the Gospel and of the Apostles, the more ecumenical becomes our outlook and our approach to all ecclesiastical and practical problems. Visser 't Hooft has never tried to minimize the differences between various types of Christianity, primarily between the Catholic and Protestant structures of the Church. He has never tried to reduce the historical differences to some kind of common denominator. He has always opposed any effort to use ecumenical co-operation for the construction of a super-church. He has encouraged all ecumenical groups to come together at the depth of the burning Gospel of the Incarnate, Crucified and Risen Lord. He is a living example of the fact that a real theology must be related to the life of the Church—historically divided and diversified, but continually transformed and rejuvenated by the Word coming from above and incarnate in Jesus of Nazareth.

There is no other way to maintain a creative and serious dialogue between various churches, theological schools and movements. It does not mean ignoring historical institutions, ordinances, liturgical and sacramental orders and living traditions as they have sought to express the very substance and mystery of the Church. But it means looking beyond institutions and traditions, and guarding oneself against petrifactions as they, over and over again, threaten any church and any movement. Even the World Council of Churches, since it is an organization of official churches, lives in constant danger of institutionalism. Visser 't Hooft's theological insight, and passion for real theology, has protected him against this danger. My hope is that, when to our regret he terminates his public and official activity, his work will be crowned by the fact that the World Council of Churches will be on the move. It would be a tragedy if the Council succumbed to the sinister temptation of deadening ecclesiasticism. Just in these days, in a time of a profound transformation of contemporary mankind, this sinister temptation exists to withdraw into the ghetto either of confessionalism or of an abstract theology, both irrelevant in view of the great mission of the Church of Christ.

Looking back at the last ten to fifteen years of ecumenical activity from Amsterdam to Evanston and New Delhi, we realize more fully than we did before the depth and intricacy of the general situation of the world, and of the many dangers and perils threatening the very structure of the World Council. On two occasions it was especially tempted to act as a Western institution: first in the summer of 1950 at the beginning of the fateful Korean War, and second in the autumn of 1956 during the ominous and tragic events in Hungary. I was very critical of the way in which ecumenical leadership acted in those days. I am not, however, at all ready to blame anybody, and to pass judgment upon any of the responsible persons and groups. The complexity, and the unprecedented nature, of the post-war development of the world in general, and of the European situation, at the dividing line between the East and the West, in particular, made it almost impossible, or at least very difficult for a body like the World Council to penetrate to the very depth of the historical situation beyond the normal political

and international level. The criteria guiding thought and understanding and eventually decisions, were a heritage of a long
historical, political, cultural and moral development of Western
countries. They were almost dogmatically valid and beyond
criticism. The Western countries were regarded as the
guardians of the political and moral heritage of Christian
civilization, of all the great treasures of freedom, justice, and
political and international decency. I have a deep understanding
of many spiritual and moral values associated with what we
call Western civilization. And I am aware of many perils
connected with the present revolutionary events in the East.
My theological perspective, however, has warned me against
what we call self-righteousness, deeply rooted in all of us, and
it has opened my eyes and ears to the fact that humanity has
been finding itself in the pangs and throes of a profound
transformation, rebirth and reorganization, and that our old
criteria have lost their function and relevance. Our great
mission is to fertilize *the new level* of historic development by
what has been unforgettable and indispensable for a healthy
and creative human development.

I sincerely wish that all of us in the World Council may have
a vital vision of the world situation, of the changes, of the path,
of the direction we have to take, and of the far away and still
near horizon. What a wonderful opportunity we all have!
Eastern Orthodoxy has become part and parcel of the
ecumenical movement. East European churches may open
effectively a new view of the problem of the Church, of the
revolution and the new socialist and communist society. As
long as the old Western churches are unable to visualize a living
Church on the level of socialist society or of communist order,
the ecumenical movement will be continually weakened by the
malady of suspicion, distrust and fear. We know our difficulties
and dangers, but, in our countries, they cannot be overcome
by any Western recipe. They can be overcome only by a
profound understanding of the Gospel, by our inward rebirth,

22

by our real fellowship in repentance, love, hope and faith, by our adequate, fearless, courageous understanding of the historical changes and by our priestly compassion for the men living close to us, toiling, building, suffering, hoping, no matter whether these men are believers or unbelievers. The Gospel of Jesus of Nazareth has always been a great venture with many risks and unforeseen dangers. But there is nothing more glorious, fascinating, overwhelming, and more creative, than the Gospel of the Living Lord in the midst of toiling, rebellious suffering and struggling humanity.

May I end with some personal words addressed to my friend W. A. Visser 't Hooft? The years still at your disposal as General Secretary of the World Council of Churches are few. But they may prove to be of a decisive nature for the ecumenical movement. You can implement your great mission if you walk in the path of our Lord: as servant, forgetting yourself, identifying yourself with the limitations, weaknesses, failures and shortcomings of all churches belonging to the World Council, understanding the needs and aspirations of mankind today, and transcending all the limitations of a purely confessional, parochial, national and traditional mind. Your task is not easy. And we, your devoted friends, are ready to assist you whenever you need our help and counsel. You have your own inner circle necessary for the type of work laid on your shoulders. But do not forget that there are numerous friends and brethren beyond that inner circle who are thinking of you, praying for you, and devoted to you in love and gratitude.

CRISIS AND RENEWAL IN THE STUDENT WORLD

Suzanne de Diétrich

'WHEN Friedrich Nietzsche, nearly half a century ago, exclaimed, "Hail to us, woe to us, the frost breaks!", he was generally taken for a rather interesting sort of pessimist crank. It is not through any particular perspicacity on our part that we can understand his meaning somewhat better than his contemporaries. We have witnessed the melting of glaciers and the roaring down of avalanches. The signs of the times have spoken so eloquently to us that we cannot help becoming aware that there is something the matter with our world. We do not need the gift of the prophet but rather the gift of the parrot to speak of the crisis of our civilization.' These lines were written in 1931 in the preface to a little booklet published under the auspices of the World's Student Christian Federation, called *A Traffic in Knowledge*.[1] Their author was W. A. Visser 't Hooft. In another writing of the same period he develops the same thought. After analysing the 'false gods of the West',—namely nationalism, class, technology and economies, he concludes: 'Yes, the thawing wind dissolves the comfortable structure of our Christianity; it threatens our pseudo-certainties; but it also blows on the new systems which thought of themselves as solidly built and

[1] SCM Press 1931.

24

unmasks the cults of the new gods. And all things are carried
away under our eyes by the flood. . . . Time has come for
us to say, not "Woe to us" but "Courage! The thawing wind
blows!" For where all flows away like an ephemeral river the
question of eternity, the real problem of life comes to the
fore . . . thus secularism becomes a promise. The Holy God
delivers us in the great distress of this day from all that which,
in Christianity and outside Christianity, was still faith in our
selves, in human forms, concepts and absolutes. Thus the
whole place is made free again for God.'[1] To some people
such statements may sound romantic. Did the crisis of the
thirties really have such a significance in the history of the
world and of Christianity? It will be the attempt of this essay
to analyse *some aspects* of that period, namely to see it through
the eyes of the men, all in their thirties or early forties, who
from 1929 onwards held leading positions in the student world.

The first question they felt bound to raise was whether they
still had a common message to proclaim to the world of their
day?

Such a question was never raised in the early days of Federation history. But the World's Student Christian Federation had
become with the years an ecumenical body submitted to all the
cultural, racial, national and, still more, theological and
confessional tensions of its time. It is in this sense that it had
become a true mirror of the crisis and hopes of the Church
universal which it claimed to embody in the universities of the
world. It is in this sense also, with no claim to uniqueness, that
we shall make a large use of Federation material. In the ten
years during which W. A. Visser 't Hooft was its editor,
The Student World truly reflects the movements of thought of
those times. We see students, the world over, submitted to the
struggle of conflicting ideologies, searching for new ways; we
hear of theological and biblical renewal; and, as a result of both,
we see Christians attain a new consciousness of the nature of the

[1] 'Dieu et les dieux de l'occident', *Foi et Vie*, May 1931.

Church and of the scope of her mission in and to the world.

Our Chinese friends often liked to remind us that the Chinese word for crisis is made of two signs, one meaning 'danger' and the other 'opportunity'. To use W. A. Visser 't Hooft's expression, man's failure leaves the place 'free for God' (but let us never forget that, where one devil is chased out, seven others may come). It is on the background of the crisis that we can fully grasp the significance of the renewal.

The Crisis of the Nineteen-Thirties

The 'twenties had been chaotic years. The younger generation reacted violently against its elders who had brought about the First World War. The will to live and enjoy life gave birth to romantic Youth Movements in Central Europe, while American Youth dreamed of a world free from war and oppression. In the Far East the imperialism of the West was denounced with unprecedented violence and the meeting of the World's Student Christian Federation in Peking in 1922 gave birth to a counter-movement which was openly anti-Christian and pro-Marxist. In India young people followed with enthusiasm Gandhi's movement of passive resistance. Yet in the late 'twenties it looked for a while as if the world were going to revert to old ways. 'The year 1927 belongs to a time when people the world over could again breathe freely after the fever of wars and revolutions. Men tried to forget the past and to convince themselves that a better future awaited them. European politics seemed to have attained an era of reconstruction. Stresemann and Briand reconciled Germany and France in the course of diplomatic luncheons. Capitalism seemed solidly entrenched in its positions. The different monetary systems had been stabilized and everywhere an ardent economic activity tried to regain the ground lost in war time. Henry Ford was looked upon as a prophet. In Christian circles the Conferences of Stockholm, Lausanne and Jerusalem initiated new progress. The pessimistic forecasts of a decline of the West seemed forgotten. Communism seemed far away and the Russian experience too restricted to be considered as a warning or a threat.'[1]

Then came the great economic depression. In 1934 the Director of the International Labour Office described the crisis as 'a turning point from which there is no retreat'. Systematic collective planning and action imposed itself on a world where the depression of one continent could mean unemployment and starvation for millions of men all over the world. Students were part and parcel of this crisis. After a visit to Central and Eastern Europe the Secretary of International Student Service writes: 'It is a record of bitterness and disappointment. The splendid enthusiasm of fifteen years ago has vanished. The will for constructive action has yielded to discouragement. There are legions who are tempted by suicide. . . . Uprooted from his environment, the student finds himself isolated, penniless, hungry, ragged.'[2]

This led students to feel much more a part of society than ever before. Pierre Maury, one of the most influential leaders of the Federation in those days, writes: 'It seems that the pressure of civilization is forcing them among the masses, and that they not only accept this identification, but even desire it with their whole heart. This is due on the one hand to the overproduction of intellectuals, which condemns thousands of young men to an inevitable unemployment and a corresponding *"déclassement"*, and on the other to the merciless cruelty of our technical and capitalistic civilization, in which every one, even the most capable engineer, is no more than an anonymous and interchangeable piece of the mechanism of production, and in which the sense of utter loneliness accompanies, not merely the death, but just as much the life of the individual.

[1] W. A. Visser 't Hooft, 'Jeunesse 1927 et Jeunesse 1932', *Foi et Vie*, Sept. 1932.
[2] Quoted by W. A. Visser 't Hooft in *Students find the truth to serve; the story of the WSCF, 1931-1935*, p. 12.

Overwhelmed by these "forces without a face", intellectuals, just as much as other young people, seek in the fellowship of the masses that vital human warmth which has disappeared from our bourgeois society.'[1] Visser 't Hooft notes both the willingness to serve, the readiness to sacrifice and on the other hand the 'crudity of judgment and brutality of action', 'the lack of respect for the convictions of others' which characterize these mass movements. 'One need not be an adherent of historical materialism as a generally valid explanation of history in order to admit that, in the last few years, all of life, including religion and culture as well as social relations and politics, has been coloured and deeply affected by the catastrophic happenings in the economic realm.'[2]

We have quoted extensively from this 1935 report because it is against such a background that one can understand the amazing response of young people in general, and students in particular, to fascism in Italy, and to nazism in Germany as well as the growing attraction of communism in the Far East.

In October 1930 S. K. Datta, on his return from the Far East, notes the profound changes which are taking place in regard to the influence of Christianity, as a consequence of the world war. It was believed that the primacy of the West was due to Christianity; now that belief was shaken. In China it had been looked upon as 'the Gospel of success'. In Japan the first leaders of the labour movement had been Christians, like Kagawa. But now 'the old leaders are becoming discredited, for social thought among the labour mass is outrunning the ideas of social welfare for which these Christian leaders have been responsible.'[3]

In the same number of the *Student World* we find a description of the Anti-Christian Movement in China. The society formed in Tsing Hua University calls itself 'Christianity

[1] *Students find the truth to serve*, pp. 12-13.   [2] Ibid., p. 11.
[3] S. K. Datta, 'Christianity in the Far-Eastern Disruption', *Student World*, 1930.

Eradicating Youth'. 'We not only wish to eradicate Christianity from Tsing Hua, but also from the whole of China. Yea, not only from China, but also from the whole world. Our action is entirely motivated by the urge of conscience and reason.' Why this hostility?—'In feudal society Christianity accomplished its function by means of "the will of God", "heaven and hell", "last judgment" and other similar ideas. Now it talks about "peace", "humanitarianism" and "non-resistance". How elastic a religion it is, but all the time, with only one object, viz. to oppress the people.'

On the 18th of September 1931 Japan invaded Manchuria. Fifty thousand students went to Nanking to require a declaration of war. Feelings ran high. The younger generation searched more and more for radical solutions. After a visit to China in 1933, William Martin, of Geneva, writes: 'On at least two occasions Christianity has had a chance in China and has missed it. Today there seems to be a third chance. Will Christianity fail again? There is reason to fear that it will. . . . Our Christian civilization today rests on an internal contradiction. It contains many elements of Christianity and yet it is no longer Christian. This is why it is in danger of missing this unique opportunity, which seems to offer itself, of conquering the world.' He notes that the majority of the men governing China are officially Christian but that Christianity 'no longer presents itself as an appeal to the poor' and that the faith of youth lies in science.[1] Both Kiang Wen Han and Y.T. Wu stress the disillusionment of Christian students, their search for radical solutions.

In the editorial of this same Far-Eastern number, Francis Miller writes:

'The judgment bar before which twentieth-century Western Protestant Christianity has been called is in the Orient. . . . The Western Christian recognizes his share of responsibility for the

[1] *Student World*, 3rd quarter, 1933: Far Eastern Number.

tremendous issues and problems which confront the Church in the East. Some of these issues are:

'The question of the primacy as between Christ and Caesar, with its corollary of the relation between the Church and the nation.

'The tidal wave of scientific materialism.

'The chasm between the ethical needs of contemporary society and the ethical resources supplied by the Christian community.

'The inadequacy of the sectarian as contrasted with the Catholic mind in the presence of a world civilization.'

We have tried to give a fair picture of the world in the thirties, as it was seen at the time by thoughtful men: a world in turmoil where new forces were at work, claiming to reshape the whole of society, and beyond that, the very mind and soul of man. The myth of a 'Christian West', of so-called 'Christian nations', was destroyed for ever and the Christian faith challenged as never before since the early centuries of her history. Where Christian ethics had been taken for granted as a common basis of behaviour (at least in principle) totalitarian systems emerged with their own conflicting standards. The consequences were soon to be seen. As Professor Max Huber was to put it in 1937, there can be no international order without a common ethos. The League of Nations had failed for that very reason.

In all this, where stood the Church? How far was it ready for new ventures? If one dares to say so, what was God doing in these fateful years for his Church and for his world?

The Way to Renewal

Nothing is more fascinating nor more mysterious than the way in which the Holy Spirit works in God's Church. Since we are not prophets we mostly recognize the marks of his work after the event. And it is probably still too early to appraise fully the significance of the events which led to the formation of the World Council of Churches. But certain converging

lines emerge and as we look at the short span of twenty years
between the two world wars we cannot but see God's guiding
hand. We find that at the very moment when spiritual life
seemed at a low ebb and the future most uncertain, God had
already prepared his 'seven thousand' scattered all over the
earth. At the appointed time they were to find each other, to
become aware of a common call and a common purpose.

Several converging movements prepared the way for the
formation of the World Council of Churches. In addition to
the official ecumenical movements of which the history has
been told more ably elsewhere, we see a wide group of men
and women, those who have emerged from youth and student
movements, increasingly involved in the search for more
authentic Christian witness and Christian unity. A certain
'meeting of minds' had to be achieved if the new institution
was to be, not just one more organization, but a dynamic and
creative force. This meeting of minds proved possible in 1938.
It remained possible in 1948, in spite of the Second World
War, and this is remarkable. But it is our conviction that it was
not yet possible in 1920. To understand the change we have to
turn to the crisis of the thirties and its spiritual significance. But
the crisis alone could have shown no more than God's judgment if by God's grace it had not coincided with, as well as
called forth, a deep theological and biblical renewal.

A comparison between the state of mind of Christians during
the two world wars shows a striking contrast: in 1914-18
nationalism ran so high that even devout Christians seemed to
have lost any sense of allegiance to the Church Universal.
Thank God there were exceptions; young men in the trenches
celebrated with more fervour than ever the Day of Prayer of
the World's Student Christian Federation. In 1940 the atmosphere was different; the real front was ideological and it was
with a sense of deep suffering that brother fought against brother.

In the 'twenties the gap had proved even more theological
than political. A German could raise the question in 1920, 'Do

we still serve the same Christ?' The young generation of Christians reacted against its elders; the young men back from the trenches were more interested in building world peace than in discussing 'sin' and 'salvation'. The Germans sought refuge in eschatology. American idealism seemed to them to be sheer humanitarianism (and sometimes it was!).

Evoking his first ecumenical experience in 1930 Oliver Tomkins could write a few years later:

> 'That was in the glorious days when Americans, on the crest of 1929 boom, felt they were "bringing in the kingdom of God" at unprecedented speed; when the voice of Karl Barth first came booming across Europe, not very distinct, but already uncomfortably insistent on such things as sin; when the British on the whole had American ideals but were increasingly prepared to dress them in the decent clothes of evangelical language; when the Russian Orthodox were for most still just interesting refugees, who had a bewildering habit of lapsing into obscurantist affirmations about the faith and the Church! Groping for an "emphasis" was certainly about all that could be expected from a group like that, and "oecumaniac" was a fitting pun to express the lunacy of trying to do it at all. But the necessity to try was inescapable. When we prayed together, heard the Bible together, listened to the Faith expounded, we *knew* that beneath all differences it was the same Lord who had called us. In that paradox lies the command and the task of oecumenism. Oecumenism is our answer to the Divine imperative to realize the unity we cannot express.'

We have already seen that the first action of the new team which took charge of the WSCF in 1929 was to call a 'commission on the message'. Members of this commission were F. A. Cockin, S. K. Datta, P. C. Hsu, Pierre Maury, Reinhold Niebuhr, Father Zenkovsky, W. A. Visser 't Hooft, secretary. A meeting of twenty-five leaders took place in Zuylen in 1930. Among them, older in years but not in spirit, was Dr Oldham. 'Our task', writes Pierre Maury, 'is to be true, in a new, actual, contemporary way, to the message eternally given by God . . . The message is always Jesus Christ!

. . . God's message to the Federation struck me forcibly as a great call to be *men* in the fullest sense'. 'Our world is undoubtedly terrible . . . but how magnificent and how inspiring it is to live in! How uplifting it is to love it! Even in its misery it preserves, by that very quality, the image of the God who created it. . . . I have often thought that the great phrase 'God so loved the world . . .' did not imply merely this suffering compassionate love, expressed in the Christian salvation, but also that creative love, of which we get some slight idea from the joy which breaks forth in the great artist. But it is undoubtedly still more inspiring to live in this lost world because it is a *saved* world, the world which belongs to the risen Christ, the world in which Easter always signifies the victory of God.'[1]

The 'meeting of minds' at Zuylen was not easy but the very existence of the Federation was seen to be a gift of God. The very need of the world gave new depth and breadth to the call: 'Did we not feel that we should lose our own souls unless we could believe in the salvation of the world?'[2] It was Pierre Maury's deep conviction that God's redeeming act embraced all men and the whole creation. This enabled him to be both radical in his view of the 'lostness' of man and joyfully certain of Christ's ultimate victory. The love of God could not but have cosmic dimensions. This Christocentric view of the world and of history was to be more and more the central message of the new theology of which Karl Barth was the initiator and main figure. It has been said that Protestantism in our century has rediscovered the message of Colossians and Ephesians as the Reformation of the sixteenth century had rediscovered Romans. Indeed Barth had started with Romans! but he did not stop there. The proclamation of the lordship of Christ over all realms of life meant that no aspect of daily life, in home and factory, in economics and politics, in art and

[1] Pierre Maury, 'The message of the Federation', *Student World*, 2nd quarter, 1931.
[2] Ibid.

science could be ignored. All things took their ultimate significance in God's creative and redeeming action as revealed in Christ.

This message came as a gift of God, at the very moment when totalitarian systems tried to circumscribe the Christian message to the sphere of 'private life' or tried to make use of the Church for their own purposes; at a time when the Marxist interpretation of history attracted thousands of young people, East and West. This all-embracing vision of God's purpose for his world necessarily implied a new vision of the mission of the Church. The Church had stood all too long on the defensive, abandoning sphere after sphere of life to the secular world. She had now to stand up and claim the whole of life for Christ with joyful boldness. But in a world where the sole unifying factors seemed to be technology, economics and science, how could the message of a hopelessly divided Church be heard? Only the 'Church universal' could cope with so great a task. Francis Miller, chairman of the WSCF, relentlessly pleads this cause. In a talk to American students he calls for leaders 'possessed with a passion for the ideal of the Church Universal; leaders whose intellectual powers and spiritual insight make them competent to serve not as statesmen of one denomination but of the whole Church of Christ . . . The world stands in tremendous need of persons who possess the catholic mind and spirit . . . The catholic mind has as its point of reference God as it knows him in Jesus Christ, but it also carries in its heart the hopes and sorrows of the whole world, or rather as much of the world as comes within its ken.'[1]

Francis Miller stresses the need for a dynamic lay movement of men and women who will act and think as members of a worldwide community. W. A. Visser 't Hooft insists that 'the whole significance of the movement Church-world among students is precisely that it takes its stand in the actual churches.'

[1] *Americanism and Christianity*, Addresses delivered before the National Assembly of Students, 1929.

There is a particular place in history where God has revealed himself: Jesus Christ. There is a particular place in the world where we hear his word spoken to us: the Church.'[1]

In many parts of the world students wrestled with the new ideologies and Christians had to take a stand. Enkichi Kan of Japan writes: 'The movement wanted to take up the good points of communism and combine them with Christianity. This is very easy to say but very difficult to do . . . the urgent need for us today is the strict criticism of communism from the genuine Christian standpoint.'[2]

It is in Germany that all through these years the conflict with a totalitarian ideology was to become most acute and to take its full significance. An overwhelming number of students belonged to the Hitler movement, already in 1932. The German SCM had behind it a strong pietistic tradition but under the influence of its chairman, Reinold von Thadden and of its General Secretary, Hanns Lilje, it had taken a new turn. Both were deeply committed to the ecumenical cause. Hanns Lilje in his lectures to University students knew how to tackle the contemporary problems in the realm of both philosophy and technology and presented the Christian message in challenging terms. He was to be arrested a few years later, the main argument being that too large crowds came to hear him! Reinold von Thadden, one of the greatest among the laymen of our time, was to be one of the firm pillars of the Confessing Church. His later activities in the World Council of Churches and as founder of the *Kirchentag* are well known.[3]

The tension was not only between the Church and the Nazi régime but between the so-called 'German Christians' and the 'Confessing Church'. The Barmen confession (1934) proclaimed with clarity the Christian position concerning the uniqueness of the biblical revelation. The whole resistance of the

---

[1] 'The Church', *Student World*, 2nd quarter 1932.
[2] 'The End of the Bourgeois', *Student World*, 4th quarter, 1932.
[3] See the biography by Werner Hühne, *A Man to be Reckoned with*.

Confessing Church was grounded in the Bible and this led to a far-reaching renewal of biblical theology, to a new type of commentaries, exegetically solid but speaking to the actual situation. The Word of God became once more the iron ration of the average Christian for his daily life. The influence of this renewal spread far beyond German borders and prepared other Churches for the struggle which was soon to befall them too.

In 1937 W. A. Visser 't Hooft called a conference of students in Bièvres, exclusively devoted to the Bible. It was a new venture for the Federation. This is how he summarized the experience:

> As we struggled together to understand the Bible, new light broke forth from the Word; thus Bièvres became an experience of renewal of life. How did it happen? I believe that the important point is that we did not take for granted that we knew the Bible, but worked hard for a new understanding of *the Bible as a whole for our life as a whole*. Much of the wide-spread discouragement with respect to Bible study is due to the fact that we ask first of all: how does this or that passage apply to my situation or to this or that world problem? instead of asking first: what does this mean and what does it have to say about God. The alternative is not whether we read the Bible 'piously' or 'historically' or 'critically' but whether we read it *egocentrically* or *theocentrically*. . . . But that means hard work! It was one of the joys of Bièvres that all were willing to pay the price.

Two years later the World Conference of Christian Youth in Amsterdam devoted the whole morning to Bible study, dividing into fifty study groups, and this was found to be the most constructive element in the Conference.

The biblical renewal led continental theology to an intensive study of the New Testament concept of the Church. Nineteenth-century Protestantism had suffered from an excess of individualism. The Church had all too often been conceived as an assembly of like-minded people who gathered for common worship and service. But the doctrine of the New Testament was of a community called into being by God himself as the Body of Christ carrying on his work on earth, testifying to him by its corporate existence, as well as its proclamation and service to the world. This was of course sound old Calvinist doctrine but it had been long forgotten. Its rediscovery was going to put the dialogue between the 'catholic' and the 'protestant' wings of the Church on a new level. And, at the very time when Protestantism rediscovered the Church, Roman Catholicism began to re-emphasize the study of their Bible.

In the 'twenties students were in violent reaction against all organized institutions, the Church included. In the 'thirties there are many signs of a new understanding not only of 'the Church universal'—because this could still be a way of escape from concrete commitment—but of the *existing churches*. Missions to foreign lands had also been under the fire of harsh criticism. In 1935 the Federation, for the first time in its history, called a conference completely centred on the missionary enterprise. All the problems confronting modern missions were frankly discussed by men such as Kraemer, Oldham, Larssen and others. Dr Oldham insisted on the need for a 'Church-centric approach' to modern problems; on the importance for mankind of the existence of a society which has its origin and existence not in the choice and will of men, but in a supernatural redeeming act of God; a society 'whose controlling passion and central bond and fundamental purpose is worship;' a society which witnesses to the true nature of community; a 'community in responsibility;' a redeeming community, whose purpose is change; a universal society. 'It is a community of ordinary men and women manifesting the fruits of the Spirit and pursuing their ordinary tasks and fulfilling their ordinary human responsibilities in the power of a new life, in the strength of a great hope and in the inspiration of a living fellowship.' Do we not have here in a nutshell the vision and programme of the future *lay movements* of which Dr Oldham was to be one of the sponsors?

Commenting on the Basle Conference Visser 't Hooft wrote: 'On no point was there more emphatic agreement than on this one, that the right understanding of missions is bound up with the right understanding of the Church Universal . . . It is in the setting of a world-wide Christian community in which national differences are not wiped out but transcended that we get the right perspective for the main problem of missions, namely: how can a Church become truly indigenous and still remain part of the wider catholic community of Christ's body? Again it is in such a framework that we see our own troubles—whether they are due to missionary conservatism, to colonial imperialism or to superficial syncretism—as aspects of the troubles of the Church as a whole and are thus forced to look at causes rather than effects.'[1]

Outward pressures have forced the churches to overcome their provincialism and begin to think in world terms. But, as J. L. Cottle puts it: 'Ecumenism is not founded on panic . . . Our real reason for uniting the universal Christian Church is a new vision of the character of God. We see that Christian unity does not lie in our ability to sign a common formula of belief and action, but in God's choosing us all for the accomplishment of his purpose, and in our gratitude to him.'[2] We have seen how this new awareness of the nature and mission of the Church imposed itself as a compelling call from God on an increasing number of men and women. The barriers to be overcome were of many kinds: race, class, nationalism, cultural and theological cleavages. There is no year when *Student World* does not wrestle with one or more of these issues. But they are live issues. Special conferences are called where the conflicting parties meet in thorough and frank discussion: Americans and Europeans, Bantu and Afrikaans in South Africa, Japanese and Chinese in the Far East. It is a process of

[1] 'Missions tomorrow', *Student World*, 4th quarter, 1935.
[2] 'The Christian Community in the modern world', *Student World*, 4th quarter, 1937.

give and take, of loyal confrontation which leads not necessarily to agreement but at least to mutual esteem and respect of the other's position. This is 'ecumenism lived'. But we have still to speak of one sphere in which pioneering work was done in the 'twenties and 'thirties, namely that of interconfessional contacts.

The Way to Unity

Looking back at a distance on those years, we are aware that one of the great events of that time was the Russian *diaspora*: an *élite* of Russian thinkers such as Berdyaev, Bulgakov, Arseniev and many others took refuge in France or Germany. The West became aware, after centuries of separation, of the treasures of Eastern Orthodox worship and tradition. Challenging debates took place in the Latin Quarter between Greek Orthodox, Roman Catholic and Protestant professors. Tripartite conferences of Christian students were started in France and in South Eastern Europe. Anglicans and Russians started the 'Fellowship of St Alban and St Sergius.' The Orthodox conception of the Church came as a challenge to Protestant students: a faithful Orthodox could not study the Bible without consulting the tradition of the early Fathers (how strange this sounded to Protestant ears!); he could not conceive of a student group without some corporate liturgical service. This forced the Federation, after much debate, to accept the existence of confessional groups within its fold. When in the 'thirties more and more churches launched denominational groups, they learned to work side by side in the same national Federation, the danger remaining sometimes of an 'ecumenism at the top' which did not manifest itself as constructively as one might have hoped at the local level.

Parallel to the Commission on message, a Commission on ecumenism had been formed to deal with all these issues, under the leadership of H. L. Henriod. In 1932 a conference of a rather exceptional character took place in a little village of Lorraine. The group included Roman Catholic priests, leading

Orthodox men such as Nicholas Berdyaev, Professor Zankov from Sofia, and Leo Zander; on the Protestant side there was Pastor Boegner and officers and leaders of the Federation, from five continents! An Anglican, Father Hebert, led a day of retreat. The theme of the conference was the Incarnation. The spirit was remarkable. When the Benedictine monk very tactfully expressed the desire of his heart that all could enjoy the fullness of his own tradition, no one could feel offended. Such encounters were still to be handled at that time with great discretion, but we look back thankfully to those days and see in them a sign and token of things to come. We were able to pray together and we learned to listen to one another. It was much more than an intellectual discussion: an encounter '*en Christo*'.

The most acute problem in ecumenical meetings is always the problem of common worship and intercommunion. The publication of the hymnbook *Cantate Domino* in the 'twenties, of the book of prayers *Venite Adoremus* in the 'thirties enabled students, and many others with them, to enter more deeply in one another's ways of worship. The suffering of not being able to break the bread together at the Lord's table made them more conscious of the sin of division. The question was sometimes raised whether it was right to attend a celebration in which you could not fully participate. Leo Zander liked to say that it was at the moment when he saw his Protestant friends communicate that he recognized his brothers in Christ in them—even if the service was heretical! It is when we stand together in the presence of Holy God that we meet at the deepest level.

Delegates from China or India criticized with some bitterness our western divisions; the Chinese told us that there were about 300 churches or sects with missions in China. How could such a divided Christ be taken seriously? Already in those days the most pressing and impatient call to visible unity came from the so-called Younger Churches.

What conclusions can we draw from this brief survey?

We have used the Christian student body as a kind of mirror in which the turmoils and the hopes of the 'thirties were faithfully reflected. There is no burning issue in the world or in the Church which has not been raised at some point in the columns of *Student World*; communism and capitalism, nation and race, the vocation of the laity, the relation of men and women, the Bible, the Church, Missions, all these themes are tackled; every year some part of the world is specifically studied, in relation generally with some meeting in this area. And all through we have seen how a new consciousness of the mission of the Church in and to the world, at home and abroad, a new thirst for unity developed. More important still—the Church was seen again as the God-given reality which transcended all the shortcomings of the historical churches, for humble allegiance and service. The unity of the Church had to be manifested 'that the world may believe'.

'Only a united Church would be able to give a fully adequate demonstration of the meaning of the Church, as in it there would be the full fellowship of witness and of sacraments in common. It is possible that the oecumenical movement in the present situation may be little more than an international humanitarian organization. It is also possible that, though it is not the Church of Christ in its fullness, it may be an "earnest" of the Church of Christ which is in the Churches, and is more than the churches.'

Thus wrote W. A. Visser 't Hooft in 1937.[1]

Oxford and Edinburgh 1937 were to be a great turning point in the history of the ecumenical movement, and the General Secretary of the WSCF was soon to become the General Secretary of the World Council of Churches in process of formation. Here our part of the story ends.

Some decades ago, a German theologian prophesied that

[1] *The Church and its Function in Society*, ed. by W. A. Visser 't Hooft and J. H. Oldham, 1937.

41

this century would be 'the century of the Church'. At first sight the crisis we have described and which has been steadily going on is a serious challenge to such a statement. The secular historian, looking at the twentieth century will see tremendous forces at work, reshaping the political and economic structures of the world. He may well look at our time as marking the end of the 'Christian era', this term describing the hegemony of a Western civilization rooted in the Christian tradition, steeped in the Graeco-Roman culture. In all this the secular historian may be right. But it is given to the Christian to see 'the other history within history', namely the one *God* writes. As we look back, above the many voices of a world in turmoil we hear the voice of Holy God calling his Church to a new awareness of her calling, to new forms of witness and service, to a new consciousness of her essential, God-given unity.

These are times of sifting and judgment. The Lord of the Church has allowed it to be deprived in many parts of the world of the earthly power it retained. It is thus reminded that it is the Body on earth of the Suffering Servant, called to share in his rejection and to be spent and broken with him, in him, if it is to triumph with him. 'Not by might, nor by power but by my spirit, says the Lord of hosts.'

Indeed 'the thawing wind blows!' But the Spirit broods on the waters and *God reigns*.

THE GROWTH OF UNITY

Henry K. Sherrill

T HE World Council of Churches has not as yet been granted in the providence of God the great miracle of a reunited Church, but nevertheless miracles have taken place. One of the most striking of these has been the remarkable spirit of understanding, of mutual respect and of friendship which has developed among the many participants in the life and work of the Council. When the first Assembly met at Amsterdam in 1948 so far as the composition of the membership was concerned the scene on the day of Pentecost seemed to be repeated in modern terms—'Parthians and Medes and Elamites, and the dwellers in Mesopotamia and in Judaea and Cappadocia, in Pontus and Asia, Phrygia and Pamphylia, in Egypt and in the parts of Libya about Cyrene and strangers of Rome, Jews and proselytes, Cretes and Arabians.' A small number had been working for years as a Provisional Committee and had come to know each other well. Others had attended previous conferences on Faith and Order, on the Missionary Task of the Churches and on Life and Work, but the great majority of delegates were inexperienced in such gatherings and were not acquainted with one another. It was indeed a diverse company. There were Asians, Africans, Europeans, and Americans. There were Orthodox, Anglicans, and Protestants of every shade and variety of opinion and

43

The Sufficiency of God

practice. Many nationalities were represented and the tensions of the recent World War were still acute. Theological convictions ranged, let us say, from the Salvation Army and the Quakers to the Orthodox. It was my privilege to attend the meetings of one of the sections. It was interesting to hear the interchange of opinions between world-famous theologians but the net result was not encouraging for the future, for as I recall it no agreement was reached as to the meaning of the word 'Creation'! In the assembly there were widely diverse economic views expressed. This could reasonably be expected but considerable agitation resulted in conservative circles, particularly in the United States. A difference of opinion arose as to the size and scope of the future operations of the Council. Because of the post-war situation it was apparent that even for a moderate budget the main support must come from the churches in the United States. Some were opposed to this prospect, fearing that as a result representatives from the United States would attempt to dominate the decisions of the Council—a concern happily not borne out by succeeding events. So we met, some upholding the authority of Tradition, others that of the Scriptures. Costumes of the delegates were varied as their opinions and backgrounds.

With such an assembly it was an inspiring morning when the proposed Constitution of the World Council of Churches was adopted at a session chaired by the Archbishop of Canterbury. There were many prayers of thanksgiving offered throughout the Christian world with wide press acclaim as if the final goal had been achieved. But realists knew that this was but the beginning and that severe tests lay ahead. I served on the Nominations Committee, of which Dr Brilioth, then Bishop of Växjö, was the chairman. It was our task to nominate the members of the Presidium as well as almost one hundred members of the Central Committee. It was time-consuming work, involving consultations with the leaders of many delegations, the balancing of geographical and ecclesiastical

44

considerations, and all from scratch. Here out of the variety and complexity of the General Assembly were to come those who were to be responsible for the work of the Council during the vitally important next six years. Certainly no one at this point could confidently predict how matters would work out.

The Assembly was most fortunate in the election of Dr Visser 't Hooft as General Secretary, but more about him later. It was his primary responsibility to enrol a staff representative of the membership of the constituency of the Council and possessed of wisdom and of consecration. The salaries were inadequate and the demands were great but the General Secretary accomplished the task with acumen and imagination. The World Council of Churches was on the way.

It would have been a simple solution for the Council to adopt a programme of theological conferences and to be content with that. I do not minimize for one moment such gatherings. But the leaders of the Council could not turn aside from the tragic events of the times. Always there has been this realism in the conduct of the Council's affairs. The plight of many thousands of refugees cried out for the churches to do something at once in the name of Christ. Many of the churches throughout the world were in a desperate situation due to the war and the aftermath. Buildings had been destroyed and financial resources were almost non-existent. At once the Council engaged in the task of the resettlement of individuals and families and of inter-church aid. This practical outreach of Christian compassion was of great help to many, but it also profoundly influenced the inner life of the Council. There could be no possible misunderstanding and controversy in the meeting of human need. Thus was born a genuine spirit of co-operative service. Furthermore the rendering of such aid brought a wide response especially from churches which had not expected such practical assistance. In this way, though not planned for this purpose, the Council made new friends as the members of the staff travelled about the world with material help but even more important with the message of Christian fellowship.

The Council was happy in the choice of the Right Reverend George K. A. Bell, the Bishop of Chichester, as Chairman of the Central Committee. He deservedly had the respect and affection of all. For many years he had been deeply involved in the Ecumenical Movement. During the war he and Mrs Bell had been of great help to German pastors oppressed by the Hitler régime, so that he was well known and appreciated far beyond the Church of England. An experienced leader in his own church, he had a sympathetic understanding of the views of those from other traditions and nations. He was a remarkable combination of gentleness and of strength. Willing to go to great lengths in the interest of co-operation, he had an unusual persistence and courage in presenting his own point of view and judgment. Perhaps all this may be summed up in the simple yet deep phrase, George Bell was a Christian. His transparent yet determined goodness was an important factor in the development of the Council.

This chapter is in no sense meant to be even a brief history of the Council. What I am interested in is the growth of a spirit of unity in a group diverse in historical background, in opinion, in ecclesiastical practice and largely unknown to one another. The fact that the Central Committee from the outset was composed largely of leaders of the churches accustomed to blaze trails rather than to follow made this task all the more exacting.

From Amsterdam to Evanston I had but small contact with the life and work of the Council. But from 1954 to 1961 I attended every meeting of the Central Committee as well as a number of meetings of the Executive Committee. I wish to write very simply as to what this experience has meant to me as an illustration of what the Council has brought to many. I do not intend to centre upon resolutions or actions but upon the underlying spiritual quality of our fellowship. Certain abiding memories will always remain with me. I think of the Sunday morning service in Davos, Switzerland, held in the village church in company with the local congregation. Professor d'Espine conducted the service in French, Bishop Dibelius made an address in German, I in English. When the Lord's Prayer was said each worshipper prayed in his own language. It again was reminiscent of Pentecost—'We do hear them speak in our own tongues the wonderful works of God.' At all the meetings of the Central Committee the daily morning and evening services were a constant reaffirmation of the unity of the Spirit. The hymns were from many traditions and in several languages. The addresses by clergymen of many churches centred on the central truths of the Christian Gospel and brought a new realization of all that we shared in common. I recall with gratitude the meditations at Nyborg, Denmark, led by Bishop Lesslie Newbigin with spiritual discernment out of his experience in India. Then there were great Sunday services. In Rhodes, the Bishop of Rhodes conducted the Liturgy of the Greek Church with Professor John Baillie of the University of Edinburgh as the preacher. I wonder if ever before a Scotch Presbyterian theologian has preached at an Orthodox service of that character and in Greece! Many of us remember the Sunday evening service in Denmark when Bishop Bell gave the sermon. We all felt that this perhaps was his final admonition to the Committee. It turned out to be so, for he died shortly after. A common worship has been the foundation stone of the Council gatherings. No one has been forced into a position contrary to his conscience or has been placed in a difficult situation. All has been free and sincere.

Yet when this has been said, I do not mean to imply that in discussions there have not been sharp, even heated differences of opinion. To meet these inevitable tensions head on and in the spirit of Christian love is one of the purposes of the Council. At Evanston there was an explosive exchange as to

47

the advisability of sending a delegation to visit the churches in the Soviet Union. While the Presidents, the Chairman of the Central Committee and the General Secretary attempted successfully in a private conference to ameliorate the situation the members of the Central Committee joined in their evening worship! The question of proselytism has created certain misunderstandings particularly on the part of the Orthodox who have strong views on the matter. Their position is so different from that of representatives of the Western churches where people in a pluralistic society are more accustomed to move from one church to another. No doubt this fear of proselytism accounted for the serious questioning by the Orthodox of the integration of the World Council of Churches and the International Missionary Council. A commission to consider all aspects of proselytism was appointed and brought in a carefully worded report which was debated at length by the Central Committee. I do not suggest that this difficult question has been finally resolved. But my point is that it was faced naturally and sincerely. Every attempt was made to understand a differing viewpoint. It is illustrative of this attitude that at New Delhi when the final action on Integration was taken the understanding Archbishop Iakovos was in the chair!

The World Council has lived in no ivory tower. The effort has constantly been made to meet the pressing problems of contemporary society. The Commission of the Churches on International Affairs was promptly created to bring the Christian conscience to bear upon world affairs. An admirable staff was secured. Well-informed Christian statements have been made at the meetings of the Central Committee in regard to the constantly recurring crises in the world. Obviously in the Committee are those of many shades of opinion. There were some representatives from churches behind the Iron Curtain. There were pacifists and those more militant with many points of view in between. Members of the Committee are of course citizens of nations with special interests. No one can be so objective as to jump out of his own skin. I recall the debate on the Cyprus issue when feeling ran high. Naturally the Greeks and the British had radically different opinions which were frankly expressed. But this debate, though tense, was conducted on a high plane of mutual consideration and resulted in the sending of a delegation to Cyprus for first-hand information and discussion with the church leaders of Cyprus. The whole complicated issue of nuclear warfare has received special attention. Of course there were many differing opinions but a unanimity was reached and the views of the Central Committee were transmitted to the nations involved. So I could continue indefinitely for nothing human is alien to the Gospel of Christ and thus to the World Council. The race question has been given great consideration, and again a delegation from the World Council was sent, this time to South Africa. The Conference from all reports was most worthwhile but certain South African churches withdrew from the Council. For this action I have heard many expressions of regret but none of recrimination. The picture I would draw of the Council is a group facing squarely the tensions and diffi-culties of the modern world, without self-interest and desiring only to serve the furtherance of the Kingdom of God.

How has this unusual atmosphere of Christian understanding come about so quickly considering the many centuries of misunderstanding, even of suspicion? It is far from my intent to imply that those associated with the work of the Council are a special group of saints. Such a claim would be pretentious and unreal. But it is true with all manifest shortcomings that there is on the part of all a sincere and single-minded dedication to Jesus Christ as Lord. The presence and voices of representatives of the younger churches have made a great contribution to this. We from an older tradition and practice so often take much of our faith for granted. Those who come from areas in which Christians are greatly outnumbered and some of whom have come to Christianity through recent conversion have a deepened sense of what Christ means to them and to the world. When I think of representatives of these younger churches I am reminded of the late Rev. Peter Dagadu, a Methodist from Ghana. Whenever he conducted the brief devotional service at a meeting of the Executive Committee I found myself profoundly moved. There was a depth of conviction which shone in his face and was marked in his words and voice. The wide geographical, racial and ecclesiastical composition of the Council could not help but make us conscious of the fact that God so loved the *world*. In this company he could not be regarded as the property of any one nation or church, and we were lifted out of our own local and partial viewpoints into the Presence of a God to whom even the nations were a very little thing. I have often said that one of the chief difficulties of the churches is that too many Christians have great convictions about little matters. The World Council by its very nature has been forced to face large issues, many of them impossible of immediate solution. To talk with Germans both from East and West Germany about their situation was a sobering experience and brought home poignantly the suffering of many of our brethren in their loyalty to Christ. To meet with Asians who have made a great sacrifice to be Christians caused a realization that the Way of Christ means often heroism and demands courage and constancy. The presence of representatives from Communist-dominated countries made plain the tragic division in the world today. One could not meet with such a group without being made aware anew of the complexity and the intensity of the race problem. The magnitude of these issues drove the members of the Council to a dependence upon God's grace. With God all things are possible. With this background of human perversity the life, teaching, Crucifixion and Resurrection of Jesus Christ stood out in clearer focus. The age-long question, 'Who shall deliver us from the body of this death?'

pressed home with new intensity. In the fellowship of the Council, Jesus Christ stood clearly as the final answer. I am always inclined to act against my environment. Sweeping assertions, however well intended, make me think of all the reasons *not* to believe them. In ecclesiastical gatherings I feel less ecclesiastical. Conventional piety puts me into a spiritual tailspin. Of course in any gathering, religious or secular, there are bound to be some expressions which are unwise or sententious and, perhaps worse, boring. In any movement there comes into use stereotyped phrases which last for a time and then happily fade away. Ecumenical conversations are no exception to this rule. But I can write very sincerely that I always came away from our meetings refreshed and uplifted by the lives and the witness of so many who had patently found in Jesus Christ the centre of their lives.

The Council, due to its many-sided outlook and composition and no doubt also because of the brevity of its years, is not tied down to stereotyped tasks and forms. There is to an unusual degree a freedom of movement under the guidance of the Holy Spirit and in the context of the changing character of the times. I would not give the impression that the Council is in any area, political, social, or ecclesiastical, inclined to the radical left. The membership is too weighted with responsible church leaders, clerical and lay, to leave the ground and to take off. There is, however, an openness of mind in group discussions, a willingness not to be bound by the dead hand of the past. The realization is apparent that ours is a Living Lord who will guide into all truth. The Orthodox emphasize the importance of tradition through the action of the early Church Councils. Many of the Europeans stress the necessary biblical basis for any contemplated action. The Americans are apt to look for the more pragmatic immediate solution. Those from younger churches and nations are inclined to be more adventurous as they face the present exigencies of their situation. These are of course only broad generalizations. Individuals cut across all classifications. But let me repeat there is an exceptional movement of the spirit in the consideration of new steps. The Commission on Faith and Order, because of the complications and magnitude of the task in dealing with the very core of the problem of Unity, makes less visible progress than committees concerned with short-range situations. The Commission itself does not propose definite proposals for unity between member churches. But the Commission affords a wide and deep background of study, knowledge and understanding which unquestionably bears fruit in the number of unions already effected and in others under consideration. In this difficult area of great sensitiveness progress is being made. New developments are constantly taking place in the areas of the role of the laity, in the place of women in the life and work of the church, in evangelism, in the study of religious liberty and of areas of rapid social change. No one in 1948 could possibly have predicted the scope of the programme. The emphasis is more upon what can be accomplished than a restatement of what has been done. In the field of action quick decisions are made. When the Orthodox churches in Istanbul were damaged in riots, at once a representative Committee was dispatched to offer spiritual and tangible aid to the Ecumenical Patriarch. When the Hungarian Revolution broke, immediately teams were on the move to the Austrian border to bring help to refugees in the name of Christ and of the Christian churches. There is nothing dead in the life of the Council either intellectually or in actions touching contemporary society. Life, interest, variety, occasionally excitement, are marks of the work of the Council. Thus there is evident, so far as one may humanly judge, the movement of the Holy Spirit. It is indeed fitting that the Presidium has chosen Whit Sunday for an annual message to the churches.

The Council is church-centred as is right, for it is a Council of *Churches*. Too often new movements are marked by sheer individualism and sometimes by an animus against the existing order with the assumption that here is a new something which will supplant the old. The Council aims to serve the churches in such an effective way that in the end there will be no council or churches but an undivided Church. A phrase often on the lips of Dr Visser 't Hooft is 'The renewal of the church'. The Council acts as a stimulus, even a gadfly, to the Christian community. Such a role is important, for the dead weight of accustomed procedure and the human failing of inertia are only too apt to slow the wheels of progress, particularly in new and uncharted paths. With its emphasis upon the tragedy of a divided Church, with its survey of the world's need and with its broad knowledge of church life both past and present, the Council does its best to protest against any ease in Zion. The recent integration of the World Council and the International Missionary Council should spur greatly the growth of missionary interest and of intelligent effort, for the missionary task is most demanding of constant revaluation in the light of changing world conditions. I have written of the dedication to Jesus Christ as a central focus in the life and work of the Council. In him is to be found the dominant urge toward unity. We speak so constantly of the Church as the Body of Christ. Today it is a broken Body. Such could not have been his purpose. The Council is aware of the ineffectiveness of the divided Church, as Bishop Azariah expressed it, 'a catastrophe' on the mission frontier. But supremely the purpose of the Council is to emphasize the will of God in Jesus Christ, that the Church may indeed be in an imperfect world a visible witness to God's truth and love.

All will agree that through the years the mainspring of the Council's thought and action has been and is the General Secretary, Dr Visser 't Hooft, who devotes himself completely to this cause to which no one can doubt he has been called by God. He possesses a great number of remarkable qualities. First of all, he is a man of convinced faith in Jesus Christ with a deep loyalty to the Christian Church. In his long experience in the student and ecumenical movements with his incisive mind, he is aware of all the frustrations and failure so apparent in the life of the churches, but he never wavers in his conviction as to what the Church can and should be. The General Secretary has dynamic energy, imagination, and an unusual quality of Christian statesmanship. He is a realist and a keen observer of world affairs both secular and ecclesiastical. A scholar in the broadest sense, he has stimulated many of the theological and intellectual pursuits of the Council. His addresses at the meetings of the Central Committee and of the General Assembly, as well as elsewhere throughout the world, have been stimulating, inspirational, and well-informed, opening new opportunities in the way of thought and action. At the groundbreaking ceremonies for the new Headquarters building, in speaking of the growth of the Council, I said that the first Headquarters had been under Dr Visser 't Hooft's hat! When the history of these formative years of the Council is finally written in the perspective of time, his gifts and contribution unquestionably will stand out as truly great. I am certain that in this sincere tribute he would not wish me to picture him, at least for the present, as a stained-glass-window saint. In making countless decisions and pronouncements in a worldwide task he is usually right but he is not infallible. He is keen, tense, and sensitive. Occasionally when steamed up he explodes. When the brief period of thunder and lightning has passed the sun shines more brightly.

The Central Committee was again most fortunate in the choice of a chairman when at Evanston Dr Franklin Clark Fry, President of the United Lutheran Church in the United States, was elected to succeed Bishop Bell. He has brought unusual gifts in his great ability as a presiding officer, decisive yet considerate, serious and at the same time witty with an ability to grasp both the major issues and the necessary minor details. Dr Fry has been ably seconded by Dr Ernest Payne, General Secretary of the Baptist Union of Great Britain and reland, as Vice-Chairman. His wisdom and poise have been of immense help. Of course these men have carried this responsibility in addition to the demanding work in their own churches in the United States and in England.

I have written of my experience in the Council in glowing terms. Perhaps some will think too much so. The Council, Central Committee and staff are made up of vital, forceful human beings. I am not unaware of the entire situation. Of course at times there are hurt feelings, sharp disagreements and disappointed hopes. The same was true of the Apostolic Church. We may be thankful that there are few automatic 'Yes'-participants in the work of the Council. Anyone who has prepared a report for the Central Committee or for any of the Commissions has been forced to learn this fact the hard way! Outspokenness is one of the characteristics of the group. But when all this has been admitted there is a deep underlying unifying experience and purpose in the bonds of understanding affection and of course the Christian Gospel. Often after a warm debate there has been a roar of laughter. As we have gathered in many parts of the world there have been afforded many opportunities for the building of close friendships. For myself, I think of sitting next to Dr John Baillie at the meeting of the Central Committee, a man of deep religious experience, of profound knowledge and of wide compassion. His witty and keen asides enlivened many a session for me. He will always remain in my life as an inspiration. The meal hours and the intermissions between sessions afforded an opportunity for informal discussion. I recall many happy incidents—I can see Dr Visser 't Hooft, completely relaxed after a strenuous day, joining in the singing of popular songs led by a Hungarian pianist. Who can forget the witty and generous speech of Archbishop Fisher at St Andrews as he spoke in appreciation of Drs Fry, Payne and Visser 't Hooft? In all the gatherings there may be found the spirit of worship and dedication, hard work involving the preparation of papers, addresses and programmes with long meetings, but also often there has been friendly gaiety—the best indication of the naturalness and the mutual trust of the participants. My relationship to the Council is over. Many of the debates have faded into obscurity but there abides the friendship of Christian men and women from all over the world, making 'From Greenland's icy mountains to India's coral strand' a great understatement.

There is of course much more to be done with greater effectiveness as the task is long and complicated. One point I would make is the advisability of enrolling more laymen and women in the Council's work. Too many official ecclesiastical leaders are involved and thus there is too great a preponderance of clergy. I think of the contribution of such laymen as Charles Taft, Francis Miller, Nathan Pusey, Reinold von Thadden, Charles Parlin, Kenneth Grubb and of course that ecumenical veteran Dr Alivisatos. This is the type of representation which is important for the future of the Council.

The impact of the Council upon the life of the churches is great. The fact that church leaders from all over the world have met in a fellowship such as I have described has created a new climate of understanding and appreciation. Such an atmosphere has made a significant if intangible contribution to discussions now in progress between many member churches. The intellectual and the spiritual life of the churches has been stimulated. But, as has been often pointed out, the influence of this ecumenical movement must be extended to reach the rank and file membership of all of the churches. By this I do not mean simply information about the life and work of the Council, though that is important. What is most needed is ecumenical action by local congregations themselves in their own communities. Still the congregations are apt to live in water-tight compartments with too little contact as churchmen with those of other communions. The whole ecumenical movement is largely confined to the leadership of the churches. This is fine as far as it goes but is not sufficient.

The World Council is in the long range of church history but an infant. But we are now entering into a time when the third generation of leadership must undertake the responsibility. There must be successors to George Bell, John Baillie and others as they followed Bishop Brent, Archbishop Temple, Archbishop Söderblom, Dr John R. Mott and their fellow-workers. The very success of the Council to date poses a problem. The World Council must never become another useful church organization living for its own perpetuity. The final goal of a reunited church must not be lost sight of in useful co-operation. The pioneers in the movement had a passion for unity as a result of their own practical experience and of course primarily because of their conviction that this unity is the will of God in Jesus Christ. Such must be the driving force in the study and work of the Council in the exciting and crucial years which lie ahead.

OBEDIENCE AND WITNESS

Georges Florovsky

IN the ecumenical movement we meet as Christians. We meet in the name of our Lord. But we meet as *divided Christians*, and we are conscious of our divisions, of our 'unhappy divisions', as the phrase goes. Moreover, we are *born* into a divided Christendom, we are involved in the Christian split before we realize it, before we are consciously aware of it. And this constitutes the major predicament of the Christian situation. Nobody wants to be a sectarian, a member of a sect. Christians want to be Christians—members of the Church, not of a sect or denomination,—of the Church, One, Holy, Catholic, and Apostolic. The problem was much easier in the age of individualism, when people could claim that religion was their private commitment, *eine Privatsache*, as it was so often contended in the last century, across various denominational boundaries. The boundaries then could be easily transcended, or rather ignored and neglected. It could be then contended that one could be a *Christian man* without being a *churchman*, in any concrete or empirical way. Unfortunately, at that time, even churchmen were often unaware of their churchmanship, which they tended to regard as something rather accidental, 'purely historical', relative, an accident of historical situation. A sharp distinction was suggested and acknowledged between *faith* (or 'spirit') and '*institution*'; and the 'institutional aspect' of the Christian commitment was regarded as accidental and optional, as something purely human, and all too human. Indeed, many Christians, and probably an overwhelming majority, still hold this position, at least for their own personal use and satisfaction, although they may readily accept the traditional discipline of their respective Christian affiliations for various reasons—convention, efficiency, aesthetic appeal, and the like. The institutional fabric of the Church is often accepted as a venerable historical tradition, which must be preserved and continued, and yet without any belief in the Church. Now this individualistic approach to the matter, which paradoxically may be combined with the strictest confessional intransigence, and even arrogance, has been vigorously challenged in recent decades. It has been said, by a contemporary Protestant theologian, that modern Christians have suddenly rediscovered the Epistle to the Ephesians. Perhaps this is an exaggeration: not all have made or assessed this discovery. Some others might have discovered the divine dimension of the Church in other ways. But the *corporate* nature of Christian existence has been increasingly recognized in these recent years. If I may be permitted a personal note, I would recall a small, but significant episode. Many years ago, in one of my articles, I wrote: 'Christianity is the Church.' At that time the phrase was singled out even by sympathetic reviewers as a 'formidable' claim, as a heavy charge. At present the phrase would pass almost unnoticed; it has become almost a commonplace. It does not mean that all implications of this elementary statement are clearly recognized, and readily accepted, by all. Indeed, the phrase itself is rather vague and ambiguous. It can easily be misunderstood and misinterpreted. It is true only in the total context, in the context of the total creed. Indeed, from the purely historical point of view it cannot be contested that from the very beginning Christianity has existed as Church, that is, as a community of committed believers, joined together not only by their common convictions, but, above all, by their common allegiance to the living Lord, by the acknowledgement of the mighty deed of God. 'The Church' was actually established by Christ Jesus himself, in the days of his flesh, even before his redeeming death. One must even claim that the Church was re-established by him, within Israel, the chosen people of the Old Covenant, as a 'Messianic community', a 'faithful remnant',—in the phrase of our Lord himself, 'the little flock', τὸ μικρὸν ποίμνιον. And this 'little flock' was organized by himself, through the appointment of the Twelve to whom 'authority' was given. The Church is ever present in the Gospels. The Four Gospels are not a book for individuals, they are rather a community book. Believers become Christians when they are incorporated into the Church. But it is at this very point that the major question arises. All that has been just said may be true as an historic fact, in the dimension of human historic reality. The Church is the historic form of Christian existence. *Unus Christianus nullus Christianus.* This has been known for a long time. But does the Church belong to the very *esse* of Christian existence, is she more than just its historic form? The psychological situation of modern Christians has been reversed. In the last century it was much easier to believe in an 'invisible Church', and to neglect her historic form and shapes. In our generation it has become difficult to believe precisely in that 'invisible' Church, to go beyond the historic dimension. The institution has become more obvious, and has a growing appeal. This statement may seem more than paradoxical. Are the historic forms really so much venerated now, in a divided Christendom? Is it not the opposite which is true? Indeed, no sweeping generalization is possible. It would suffice, however, to quote but one highly significant instance. In various modern negotiations for Christian reunion between the Protestant denominations, it has been assumed that certain historic forms of organization (the 'institutional fabric') must be restored or accepted as the

basis and bond of unity, although any theological interpretation
of these forms and fabrics should be prohibited and excluded.
I have in view the notorious case of the so called 'historic
episcopate' which is supposed to have been restored or
established, through Anglican mediation, in the newly united
'Church of South India'. The episcopate may be no more than
a purely historic institution, a bit of human tradition, without
any deeper doctrinal significance, and open to free interpretation, and yet it is taken as the basis of reunion. Much less
attention is given to the unity, or unanimity, in faith. I am
quoting this example not in order to judge the Church of
South India, which has been highly praised as a noble and
promising achievement even by some renowned theologians
in the Roman Church—with whom, for myself, I regret to
disagree. I only want to make a point: fabric is put before, or
even above, faith; or, rather, unity in doctrine is reduced to an
ambiguous minimum, but 'historic' forms are imposed. Indeed,
this particular endeavour is less paradoxical and enigmatic in
the concrete situation of the missionary churches. And in this
particular situation the whole predicament of 'divided
Christendom' becomes pathetically conspicuous. The Protestant missionaries overseas had no primary intent to convert
natives to 'sects'. They honestly wanted to gain them for Christ
and his Church. In fact, however, they were gaining them for
their *denominations*. Several separated, and often competing,
Christian bodies were established in the new lands. And this
situation practically engulfed also the missionary activities of
the Orthodox Church and of the Roman Church. 'Divided
Christendom' was expanding to the countries, in which the
reasons for this 'divided state' were unknown and existentially
unreal. It was in these missionary fields that the shameful
scandal of division became shockingly spectacular. It was in
these fields that the 'ecumenical urge' has been first felt, and the
call to unity has been heard. In the actual situation of missionary
or 'younger' churches, as they were styled, the emphasis

naturally was put on the external or organizational unity. 'Unity' has been singled out as an independent item and as a primary and immediate objective. Indeed, it was a burning issue in the missionary field. And it was assumed that witness could be reduced to the 'basic' features of the Christian message, to the 'preaching of the Gospel', of the Word.

We are brought now close to our own problem, to the problem of Christian Unity in our own situation, in our own historical perspective, in the perspective of the traditional world of Christian civilization, to which we, on the American continent, belong by heredity. We also hear the call to Christian Unity as our impending obligation, as a bounden duty. And this call is strengthened by our internal anxiety, by all sorts of fears. One cannot evade conscientiously the ecumenical problem, the problem of Christian Unity. Indeed we find ourselves in different positions, according to the character of our doctrinal allegiance. It is but natural in divided Christendom. The ecumenical problem was first formulated by the Protestants, or rather they formulated their own *ecumenical* problem, which simply does not exist for the Orthodox as it does not exist for Roman Catholics also. The basic presupposition of Protestant ecumenism is *the parity* of existing denominations, at least in certain limits which can be differently defined, against the background of a certain 'given unity', as the conventional phrase goes, which is regarded both as a gift of God and his inherent purpose. The main task is, accordingly, 'to manifest' this given unity, to embody and to expand it. This implies a kind of mutual recognition. Denominations are taken to be complementary to each other. The practical objectives can be differently defined. The first spiritual danger, implied in this attitude, is that of *ecumenical impatience*. If 'unity' is already 'given', and Christians are called to 'manifest' it, it is difficult to understand why they should postpone the most spectacular gesture which can be imagined, that is to join in an united and common act of Holy Communion. In fact, this action, under various names—inter-communion or open communion, concelebration, and the like, is constantly demanded, especially by the younger generation, as an integral element of any ecumenical action, and as a token of honesty and seriousness of ecumenical endeavour as such. The rest seems to be but idle, uncommitted talk. The *act* is wanted, an outward gesture, a *visible* sign. It is often honestly admitted that those invited to join and share may disagree profoundly and conscientiously concerning the meaning and character precisely of this solemn common action, as also concerning other basic Christian doctrines. In this situation it is difficult, for an outsider—that is, for a 'non-Protestant'—to understand what this precipitate action can really contribute to the cause of unity. The sting of disunity seems to be bluntly ignored. The existing unity—that is, the alleged 'given unity'—seems to be considered as adequate—only an outward 'manifestation' is missing—while, in fact, there is but variety and divergence. I would not deny that, in many cases, this ecumenical impatience is an honest and noble conviction. I only contend that it misses the point, ignores the problem, and aggravates confusion. It does not promote unity, if only because not all are impatient, impulsive and hasty. Indeed, those who are more sober and farsighted are often accused of lack of courage, and even of hypocrisy and doctrinairism. I am mentioning all that because it is a burning issue, precisely in youth circles. It was a major issue at the Ecumenical Youth Assembly at Lausanne in 1960. The message was delivered by youth delegates to the Faith and Order Commission of the World Council of Churches to the effect that youth regards senior leaders and theologians as obsolete and retrograde folk, engaged in vain discussions and unable to act. We were informed that youth will act without us. Of course, it was not the common opinion of the assembly, and obviously not of Christian youth at large. In any case it was an important symptom. Impatience was motivated by Christian obedience, obedience to the divine call to unity. All should be one—let us act immediately as if we were already one. It is assumed that the so-called 'given unity' is an adequate ground to stand on. The claim of obedience should be respected, of course. But should obedience be blind and merely formal? It is significant that a few years ago a regional Conference was convened in the United States, at Oberlin, Ohio, in September 1957, to discuss precisely this basic question: What is the unity we seek? And no agreement on this score has been reached. One can but conclude, reasonably and faithfully, that Christians are not yet ripe for reunion, as they are still uncertain about the nature of unity which must be sought, or, in fact, are deeply divided at this very point. Are we not just playing with an abstract concept of unity, without any definite content? It only confirms my diagnosis of the contemporary situation: people are uncertain about the 'invisible' matters of faith and are desperately concerned with outward manifestations, although it is utterly unclear, what actually they are going to manifest. I have but to add at this point that no organizational union which, by its internal pattern and inspiration, excludes all Catholic-minded Christians—using the term 'Catholic' in its widest possible sense—can claim to be 'Christian Union', or a 'manifestation' of such. It would but dig a new and deeper gulf.

The Third Assembly of the World Council of Churches at New Delhi, India, is going to discuss the problem of Christian obedience under three headings, or in three sessions: Unity, Witness, Service. I would not dare to anticipate the findings, but personally I can foretell a heated debate on all three points. Moreover, the crucial question remains: What is the true relation between the three? Can 'unity' be separated from 'witness', even for the sake of discussion? And 'witness' is witness to what? The will for unity is a noble will. And will to witness, to testify, is a good will. But one thing seems to be left out, and it is 'the only thing which is needful'—the Creed. Now, the Creed includes an article on the Church, and, in a sense, it is

its climax, the subsequent articles being its elaboration—up to
the final consummation of the hope, in the age to come. Before
we start speaking of Christian Unity, we must be clear about
the nature of the Church: Christian Unity is, indeed, the Unity
of the Church, and Unity in the Church. It may be true that
there is still no definitive and authoritative definition of the
Church. But there is the Church herself, as a divine institution,
visible, historical, and yet transcending and uniting all ages
and all stages of her historic pilgrimage in the continuity of her
being. A former bishop of Gloucester, A. C. Headlam, once
said: the Church has never existed in history, there were but
'schisms', particular bodies, divergent branches. And accordingly he pleaded for recognition of parity or equality of all
historical 'schisms', in anticipation of the coming of the
Church, of the Church to come. In fact, many people, among
the Protestants, are committed to this view. But Orthodox, as
well as Roman Catholics, are bound to repudiate this view, and
the whole approach, resolutely and comprehensively. The
starting point of their 'ecumenical engagement', as much as
they may disagree among themselves, is radically different. And
accordingly their understanding of Christian obedience, and
of the call to unity and witness, is radically different, as much
as they may, and as they should, sympathize with any honest
search and urge for Christian Unity. Indeed there is a 'given
unity', and this unity has been 'manifested' and is being
'manifested'—*in the Church itself*. But the Church is more than
just a witnessing body, as she is more than a worshipping
body: the Church herself is an integral part and subject of her
own total witness, because she is not only a body of believers,
but the Body of Christ. One may dare to say even more; the
Church is Christ himself, as he lives and rules in his own body
and its members—*totus Christus, caput et corpus*, in the glorious
phrase of St Augustine. The Church is the historical form or
modus of Christ's abiding and acting presence in the world, in
history, in the cosmos, redeemed, being redeemed, and to be

redeemed. Indeed, the Church is a historical entity, visible and temporal, a phenomenon in the human dimension. But the 'historicity' of the Church is at once also her ultimate 'super-historicity', for it is a historicity of the divine Presence. The Church indivisibly, but also unconfusedly, is both 'visible' and 'invisible'—ἀδιαιρέζως καὶ ἀσυγχύζως. She has her own structure and her own distinctive marks. But in no sense is the Church a 'denomination'. There is but One Church in history, although, unfortunately, there were many and manifold 'schisms', separated from her. This is the first presupposition of what can be called 'Orthodox ecumenism', as little as it has been practised.

It is not my purpose now to expound, even in outline, Orthodox ecclesiology. I have done so already on various occasions and cannot add much to what I have said. I want to concentrate now on the direct contribution of Orthodox ecclesiology to the methodology of sound ecumenical study and action. And I want to introduce at once my favourite idea of *'ecumenism in time,'* which I personally believe to be a right methodological key to all ecumenical locks and riddles. Indeed, it is no more than a key, a 'method', ἡ μέθοδος—the way. We may contrast this kind of ecumenism with the current 'ecumenism in space', which is in common and current practice, and which has been not unjustly, if bitingly, described as an 'exercise in comparative theology'. Usually one begins with the existing 'denominations', including the Church, in so far as she is empirically one of the existing Christian bodies, and proceeds to recording 'agreements' and 'disagreements', with the hope of discovering a certain common core of belief, which may be used as a starting point, or eventually as a basis or ground, of *rapprochement* and reconciliation. The weak point of this method is that it is basically *static* and ignores precisely the major issue: that of 'schism' or 'separation'. No 'agreement' can heal 'the schism' automatically, important and valid as agreement may be, for 'disagreements' do not disrupt communion immediately, unless they are intransigently pressed and stressed. The other weak point is this and it is difficult to say in general which of the two is more decisive: the criterion of comparison is uncertain, and usually vague. Reference to Scripture, to 'Scripture alone', *sola scriptura*, does not provide sure guidance. One cannot ignore that historical context in which only Scripture has its living voice. It is increasingly realized in our days, across all denominational limits, that Scripture (the Bible) and Church cannot be separated. The Bible itself is alive only in the Church, within the Church, that is, actually, in the context of living Tradition. One may differently determine the actual chronological date up to which one should admit the normative and binding character of tradition. Already in the sixteenth century it was strongly supposed that one should go at least up to the Council of Chalcedon (451) and to abide by the 'agreement of five centuries', *consensus quinque-saecularis*. The Orthodox would contend, of course, that one must go much further and that, in fact, there is no chronological limit at all, as Tradition is still alive and the Spirit does continually inform and guide the Church. Indeed, Tradition is not just the 'traditioning' of ancient insights or propositions. On the contrary, it is a continuous meditation on the basic events of Redemptive History, of what is still usually denoted, even in English, by the German word: *Heilsgeschichte*. And in this continuous and progressive meditation, under the guidance of the Holy Spirit, new depth and deeper meaning are discovered in what has been done and revealed by God in Christ. One should turn back and refer to Christian Antiquity not because it is ancient, 'primitive' (not in a pejorative sense, but as *Ur*geschichte, *Ur*kirche—terms not easily translatable into English), or archaic, but because it is the only method by which we can enter the living stream of the Church's life, thought and endeavour. The major predicament of modern man is that he is imprisoned in his 'modernity', and his horizon is sorely limited and circumscribed. The past has for him passed away, beyond his reach, including the *redemptive past* of the Gospel. The modern man just remembers the past, which has flown far away from him. The 'agreement of five centuries', of five centuries only, is, indeed, an inadequate foundation, if it is taken in a restrictive sense. But, for the modern man, and for us all, as prisoners of our age and 'modernity', it would be an enormous gain and a tremendous achievement if we could enlarge our vision and comprehend Scripture, that is, the primary and Apostolic witness to Christ and his decisive deed and victory, in the living context of Christian life and thought of those five great centuries—if we could identify ourselves, sympathetically and spiritually, with the generations of old, with that noble army of witnesses which deposited their testimonies through the centuries. Indeed, modern man, or rather the more responsive and sensitive man in our generation, is conscious and aware of his limitations, of his desperate insularity in an expanding universe; but he wants and attempts to overrule his insularity in space, by superadding together various *local* traditions, habits, and insights, in the manner of the United Nations or of Federated Churches. Indeed, the chains of 'provincialism', or of what is called 'parochialism', are real and heavy, and they also should be broken. But much more dangerous are the chains of oblivion, the lack of historical perspective. A secular analogy may be helpful at this point. Nobody can grasp the very meaning of his national *ethos*, unless his vision embraces the past. Nobody can be really creative, unless he is integrated in the tradition of that cultural field in which he searches and operates. Artists study the works of old masters not just as monuments of antiquity, but as testimonies of creative endeavour. Philosophers read ancient masters as testimonies of their companions in search and tasks. Those among the modern Christians who are impatient and are ready to break through all walls of partition, which, indeed, were erected in history, in the past, may be well advised to enlarge their vision and to learn from the experience of the past. Probably, this advice will not be received, but rather will be ridiculed and mocked at. But, even from the purely human point of view, it has always seemed strange to me that it is so easily forgotten that there were Christians before our own time and that their witness should be respected and carefully pondered. So much even from the purely human point of view. But by breaking through the limitations of time one can recover the sight of *solidarity* in vision and endeavour through the ages. Even this is no more than a human approximation to the mystery of the Church, which is, after all, not only an inclusive community in space, in expanding space, but even more an inclusive community in time, through the ages, because the Church is the *one* Body of *one* Lord, ever the same, yesterday, today and tomorrow—the Body to which new members are constantly added (although, unfortunately, certain members are lapsing away), until the day of ultimate consummation and of discrimination comes by the will of God in the unknown future. And there will be no time any more.

My exposition has been sketchy and rhapsodic, as usually happens with me. It is time to sum up and to relate disjointed pieces to each other. The starting point of our inquiry was *obedience*, and a call to obedience. Many of us have heard the call to work for Christian Unity and we are ready and willing to respond. Indeed, disunion is shame and scandal. I have suggested that actually we do not agree concerning the nature and the scope of Christian Unity which we want to recover, to establish, or even to enforce. The ultimate reason for this disagreement is that we differently comprehend the nature and the mystery of the Church. Now, of course, one can *discover* the Church of Christ, in the whole confusion of divided Christendom, without any technical historical inquiry. And let us bless Christ's holy name for that. But one can never *comprehend* the nature and power cf the Church, except in the

historical perspective. Because the Church of Christ, being
ever identical in her being, does nevertheless live and grow in
time, her growth must be perceived and acknowledged re-
verently and thoughtfully. My sharp strictures on what I have
called 'ecumenical impatience' are motivated and inspired by a
deep respect for human history. One cannot undo history just
by ignoring it, nor should anyone be so disrespectful of
Christian history, in all its perplexity and confusion, in its
failures and successes. One can advance only by steps and
stages. I am now concerned only with the next step, with our
immediate objective in our ecumenical conversation, which,
probably, at present cannot profitably proceed beyond the
'get acquainted' stage. And for that reason I have left unsaid
many important things which, of course, ought to be said,
sooner or later. We may be impatient to 'manifest' the
God-given unity. But are we really *in* this unity? And what is
the unity? We are impatient to witness. To witness what?
Our individual or group-convictions or opinions?—or the
Truth of God, as it has been manifested by God himself, in his
Holy Church through centuries of Christian history, and has
been comprehended, meditated upon, expounded and embodied in the lives and testimonies of the continuous series of
faithful witnesses, up to our own troubled time? Are we going
to witness in our own name or in the name of the whole body
of our fellow-brethren, from Pentecost and up to now, or
rather in the name of the Church, which is the pillar and
foundation of the truth? Obedience cannot be, and should not
be, divorced from witness. But witness itself must be a true
witness, complete and comprehensive, the witness to the 'whole
Christ', *caput et corpus*, to the whole body of Christian truth.

We are, indeed, called to till the ground, But others, before
us, have already prepared the soil. We must enter into their
labour, humbly, respectfully, patiently. *The Lord himself is
patient*, as St Paul has said.

ECUMENICAL EXPERIENCE
AND CONVERSION:
A PERSONAL TESTIMONY

Yves Congar

THOUGH this essay is written in the first person, I know that many of my friends, priests like myself, would bear the same witness, and so I feel that to some extent I speak for them. Their witness would have been better expressed than mine. If I have been kindly singled out to write these pages, it is doubtless in recognition of those first talks that W. A. Visser 't Hooft and I had in the setting and atmosphere that led to the 1937 conferences, especially that of Oxford. Since then circumstances have kept me apart from the more significant ecumenical activities. There has been no change of heart; my convictions have broadened and strengthened in line with their awakening, answering a call bound up with my progress to the priesthood.

The ecumenical dialogue has, in the first place, obliged me and helped me to renew the Christian man within me. It has, as it were, compelled me to become more Christian and more catholic. The questions put to me, the witness I have had to bear, the obligation I have been under to attain a certain level of truth, all this has shaken me from a comfortable and commonplace conformity and made me re-examine many matters in depth.

First, it has meant for me an expansion both mental and spiritual. Merely to know a foreign country does that for you especially if you speak the language. You become less provincial. The mind is, as it were, fertilized by contact with another world. For example, German language and thought have often had this effect on Frenchmen, as French language and thought also has had upon Germans. But in the ecumenical dialogue the new worlds opened up to us are spiritual worlds inhabited by other Christians. We have to get to know these worlds. Books tell us of these things, but we cannot appreciate the validity of what they say except in the light of personal experience. This experience has moreover something more to contribute than books; nothing can take the place of direct contact with living reality. It may not be necessary for such contacts to be numerous, but they are indispensable as a means of reaching authentic knowledge. I for my part shall always remember the first time I stayed in a theological college or in an Anglican religious community and the simple but lasting impression made by Evensong or Compline. Or again the first meetings between Catholic students and members of the French SCM. I know how much my understanding and love of the Orthodox Church owe to personal friendships. Father Portal, a few months before his death, bore witness to the part that 'friendship in the service of unity'[1] had played in his life and work. For all of us, the Orthodox celebration of the liturgy has opened the door to a certain understanding of the scriptural texts, and to that world of tradition and saintliness of which the Orthodox Church is the hallowed sanctuary.

The discovery of another spiritual world does not uproot us from our own, but changes the way we look at many things. For myself, I remain a Latin Catholic, a fact I do not hide from myself or from others, but ecumenism has freed me from a certain narrowness of outlook, characteristic of the Latin and

[1] Fr F. Portal *'Le role de l'amitié dans l'union des Eglises'*, a lecture given in Brussels in 1925 and published in *La Revue Catholique des Idées at des Faits*.

of the Mediterranean man by bringing me into touch with Eastern Christians, Scandinavians, Anglo-Saxons and with their respective traditions. I have kept my Latin anthropological make-up but have looked critically upon its limitations. Moreover, in and through this very experience I have learned that not a few causes of historical conflict are really matters of mental outlook, or, as I should say today, of anthropology. In *Chrétiens Désunis* (1937) I devoted much space to this theme, unaware that at the very same time a report sponsored by the Edinburgh Conference had given currency to the concept of 'non-theological factors' as causes of division, an idea of such promise for the future. Their decisive importance can be granted without failing to recognize the absolute primacy of matters of doctrine. Experience shows that ideas become deflected in different mentalities and so in vocabulary and even in their expression. And at the same time we remain closed or show ourselves open to possibilities of understanding and eventual agreement according to our disposition. Now where disposition is concerned, we are to a great extent conditioned by mentality, culture, spiritual practices and group attitudes, and the historical background of the milieu to which we belong. It is with all this conditioning that we live as Christians in the group and in the tradition where we have received it. For each of us this is something to be venerated and cherished, but like all things human it is relative, and like all historical reality, a medley, whereas Christianity on the other hand is absolute, unique and pure.

And so in the face of all this that is not the truth itself and can even prevent its diffusion, we must acquire a wholesome sense of relativity. Knowledge of others, which is only complete if it is first-hand and factual, awakens this sense. It thrives on the study and more especially the knowledge of history. I have devoted much study to history, still do and, God willing, will continue to do so. At first I had scruples about doing so, being over-concerned to remain true to the doctrinal vocation of a preaching friar of the Dominican order. I have since then realized that history is one of the best means of approach to truth and of service to that same truth. It liberates what is true from much that surrounds and even clothes it—much that is debatable, sometimes false, and prevents what is true from being admitted by concealing it. Neglecting the finer points, my experience can be summarized as follows: every time I have had a look myself, I have discovered something other than what I was told and that was regarded by this or that group as a certainty. I looked into the matter of the Great Schism, and I realized that one could not speak as if a legitimacy accepted without dispute had been, at some precise moment, rejected by Eastern Christians, who should bear all responsibility for the break. It was much more a question of gradual 'estrangement' between two different worlds. I looked into the question of Luther, whose writings I turn to, in one way or another, almost monthly. I know, alas, that Luther has still today a bad reputation among Catholics, except perhaps in Germany. I know there is some justification for this. But I also know that one does not thus do justice either to his basic intentions or to his religious thought. In fact I know that nothing really worthwhile with regard to Protestantism will be achieved so long as we take no steps truly to understand Luther, instead of simply condemning him, and to do him historical justice. For this conviction which is mine I would gladly give my life. But Catholics as a whole, and Protestants and Orthodox as well, have obviously not made experiments similar to mine: they live their religion on a plane that is more sociological than truly personal and soundly critical.

In their sociological form, the 'orthodoxies' which nourish endless controversies, prevent one from seeing and incorporating the element of truth contained in what they combat and which must be reabsorbed into that total truth in which every mind may have communion. The foregoing remark can be widely applied in the whole field where East and West, or the ancient Church and the Reformation, confront each other historically. I have long dreamt of what a research centre might be, founded by some generous Maecenas, endowed with a first-rate library, whose fortunate students, Catholics, Orthodox, Protestants and Anglicans, would be under obligation to write, let us say, a history of the papacy or of Luther, and only publishing works signed by all of them. Perhaps thus would we escape from a situation where each, against the other, holds to a truth which the other fails to recognize. But is it not just this recognition of the other's truth, this reconstruction of a total truth and this communion within, which we pursue in our ecumenical encounters, quietly and unostentatiously, yet in a way that, little by little, makes worthless polemics give way to a real consensus of opinion?

The ecumenical dialogue passes judgment also on our clerical shortcomings and forces us to be rid of them. Not being involved individually, we do not even realize how full of them we are: be it a certain complacency which thinks it has the answers to all the problems, be it an apologetic, even apostolic haste that is rather sordidly triumphant. Sometimes true spiritual depth is to be found in a mind that does not know the truth but seeks it, whereas superficiality, a lack of any serious spiritual commitment is apparent in one who goes forward armed with a ready-made orthodoxy whereby all errors are known and refuted. The whole truth is known and formulated: it is simply a question of looking out from shelf or drawer the appropriate article. . . . This little game soon proves unplayable when one enters into dialogue with a real man.

In such a dialogue, on the one hand, by listening to the other person, I am led to rediscover in the depth and fullness of my own tradition that portion of the truth that he rightly seeks to honour and that I was in danger of overlooking. On the other hand, in setting before him my convictions, I tend to present them and consequently to conceive and live them, so that they embrace what is valid in the standpoint of the other. It is not that I give in on principle to his point of view. On the contrary, I criticize it. Ecumenism is in no sense the syncretized product of Luther plus Calvin plus St Thomas Aquinas, or of Gregory of Palamas plus St Augustine. But envisaged from the theological point of view, which is our main interest, ecumenism implies a striving after two aspects of Christian truth which sometimes seem in opposition, but which should be jointly arrived at and kept together: fullness and purity.

We are compelled to take into further consideration, and to have more respect for, those points which our opponent considers we underrate. This formula often used before the 1939 war is still valid. The new development that the ecumenical movement has undergone in the World Council of Churches (characterized by the transition from 'interconfessional' relations to a dynamic community of obedience to the same call) has not robbed it of any of its fruitfulness: for one must, sooner or later, come back to moments of dialogue *between*. . . . It is a case then of each asking the other: 'Have you taken seriously this or that aspect of the truth?' For example, Protestants would say to us: 'You always give us the impression with your ecclesiastical and sacramental system of wanting to limit the operation of the Holy Spirit. Have you taken seriously God's perpetual presence? Don't you speak of grace as if it were a *Thing*, contained in a receptacle or secreted through some ritual process, whereas it is always God's initiative, his good pleasure, his promise?' And on our side, we would say to our Protestant friends: 'You always give us the impression of thinking that to attribute something to one of God's creatures as a gift from him, amounts to withdrawing it from God, who as its sole author must remain its sole possessor. Have you taken seriously God's gifts, that for us are certainties: the holiness of his Mother, ministries as an inheritance of that of the Apostles, the indefectible visibility of the Body of Christ manifest in the Church, etc?' On their side, the Orthodox would say to us: 'Have you taken seriously the active role of the whole body of the Church as such, have you, in your scholasticism, taken seriously the mystic, religious and mysterious character of religious knowledge?' And we would ask them: 'Have you taken seriously the evidence in favour of the existence of the pastoral office of St Peter as supreme and universal, an office which ensures for the Church, for the image of the Kingdom of God, the visible unity of its militant existence?'

Such mutual questioning is one of the ways by which ecumenism helps us each and all alike to make progress to-wards a fullness of understanding. Indeed is it enough to say it helps us, should we not rather say it obliges us? There exists, we believe, an ontology in encountering and in working together. Alone, I never go to the end of my own demands; I hold on to certain reserves of tolerable comfort, of a protective mediocrity. By contrast, in the presence of others, under their eye, receiving the impact and as it were the challenge of their good faith, I am forced to honour the undertaking my prin-ciples involve and to give finality to the truth which is mine. That is what one experiences in the inner councils or re-examinations of life that are part of any real community. Ecumenical encounter is the base of a similar process.

Dialogue and mutual questioning compel us by the same impulse to consider the *purity* of our Christian standpoint, for by it we are always led back to this criterion of Christian authenticity. There again, we are under compulsion, for if when alone we may perhaps allow ourselves a compromise, a certain tolerance, others deprive us of these, obliging us to verify the quality of the materials with which we work: gold and silver, or hay and straw, as St Paul puts it (I Cor. 3.12). It can come about that being with them we recognize ideas and facts that we might have been slow to rediscover alone. Personally, through ecumenical discussion or by reading Orthodox or Protestant studies, I have become aware either of certain perceptions or of certain requirements in the realm of what is specifically Christian, for example, in things eschatological. But many of my friends or colleagues tell me they have made similar discoveries directly at the source without owing anything to ecumenism. In truth, it is hard to say that one owes nothing to it, for it exerts its influence also through its promptings, by suggestion that is even conveyed indirectly and at a distance. Thus in France few priests and even comparatively few theologians have read Barth; nevertheless it is fair to ask whether the tremendous response in our midst today to the theme of the Word of God, the kind of intense and gladdening joy that so many priests today experience in their ministry, would be what it is had there been no Barth. Ecumenism, said Dom Clement Lialine, works by shock. I myself am conscious of having profited in many fields from shocks received twenty-five years ago, when, on the points at issue, I had not even had any discussion and was pursuing my quest within the framework of the Catholic tradition alone.

Dialogue indeed entails a return to one's sources. What we receive from 'the other' is a shock, but it is in our own tradition that we rediscover what was concealed there, what we implicitly took for granted, but had not clearly discerned. Later, when we have acquired a taste for it, when we have experienced the immense benefit that results from it, we make a habit on all occasions of returning to the source whence comes freshness and abundance. On the specifically ecumenical plane, however, this return to the source is possible because on the one hand we all have the same roots and come, partly at least, from the same springs. On the other hand, with this or that group, the treasure of Christianity is clothed in a certain tradition (in varying degrees of faithfulness to, and authenticity of, that tradition itself, it is true). This two-fold fact, however, provides sufficient grounds for this group and that to transcend the formulas that have been an obstacle historically, and to progress by deepened loyalty to their Christian beliefs, towards a common place of agreement. There exists therefore for both parties a possibility of living out their religious loyalty in passing beyond the sociological plane of that loyalty in order to enter into the depths of its roots and sources. Thus there is the possibility of reaching a point which could be a point of encounter. For a long time I have liked to quote, applying it specifically to ecumenism and in particular to the Catholic endeavour in that sphere, a fine passage from Etienne Gilson written concerning the philosophical opposition between Thomism and Augustinism:

'One should allow opponents whose conclusions are in conflict the necessary time to understand one another better, to understand themselves better, and to meet again at some point still today undetermined but assuredly situated beyond their present standpoints.'[1]

Where ecumenism is concerned, intellectual forces are not the only ones encountered. Each original reality has its order of existence, its laws, and so, when situated within its order, it asserts its value when experienced in accordance with its laws. That is the profound theme of Pascal's fragment on the three orders of body, mind and of charity (or wisdom or holiness).[2] Ecumenism too has its 'order' and it is felt as an authentic Christian value in an original experience which brings with it its own light and power. It is difficult to analyse an experience; one makes it. It entails a second birth, or rather it is itself a process of rebirth. One becomes thereby a different person. It is what takes place at, say, the beginning of love or when one has undergone the blessed experience of sacrifice, of the Cross, of humiliation or poverty accepted lovingly for God's sake. Or again, when in prayer one has found peace in the midst of storm, where but for prayer one would have been uprooted and swept away.

[1] '*Réflexions sur la Controverse S. Thomas—S. Augustin*', in *Mélanges Pierre Mandonnet*, Paris, 1930, t.I, p. 371.
[2] *Pensées*, L. Brunschvicg's edition, fragment 793.

The Sufficiency of God

The ecumenical climate is characterized by that fidelity in depth of which we have spoken. It calls for that readiness to go beyond which is implied in this very fidelity, and does so under the stimulus of discussion, and through the return to our sources, in the feeling that we are responding to a divine impulse in which we joyfully participate. In such a climate many things are possible which were otherwise impossible. We are living through this great moment of truth. On points on which theology had remained unyielding for four centuries, within boundaries created by polemics, hemmed in by mutual ignorance and distrust—or should I not rather say by neglect of our own deepest resources—we have begun to discover possibilities hitherto unsuspected. Works like those of H. Küng on Justification, or of M. Thurian on the Eucharist—the two most acutely controversial topics of the sixteenth century—are unthinkable were it not for the ecumenical climate and the possibilities it opens up. But one rediscovery entails another. One and all we come to a broader conception of truth. Year by year and decade after decade, we advance towards that 'point still today undetermined' of which Etienne Gilson spoke. It cannot but be very slow, for the movement must spread to the whole of theology and to all theologians. Such progress is almost imperceptible if one seeks to measure it on a short time scale. When I return month by month to the same coastline I see no change; I find the cliff apparently intact, and yet the sea is eating it slowly away. Were I to return after ten years, I would see that its outline had changed and that part of the cliff had fallen away.

Psychologically, ecumenical experience brings with it the joy of meeting, of being together, diverse and even heretical in each other's eyes, yet assembled in a similar and harmonious response to God's call. Ecumenism has no meaning and would not exist without this new factor of an impulse and call of God that will be recorded in history as one of the characteristic features of religion in the twentieth century. It is extremely difficult, perhaps even impossible, to conceive of ecumenism within the categories of classical theology alone; it is something new or, better, it is a movement, something that is not achieved, not defined, but that is daily in process of formation and definition. Ecumenism is not so much a matter in which formal revelation is concerned (except in those of its aspects which come under dogma and revealed ecclesiology) but belongs rather to the history of salvation, a free and open message from the God of Grace, translated into vocations. Work carried on in this ecumenical atmosphere is inseparable from the spiritual experience found in obedience to the ecumenical vocation. This experience is also one of a truly evangelical readiness to refuse nothing that is of God. On every page of the Gospel is a call to welcome what in man is of God or perhaps for God, beyond the limits ratified by law, beyond the categories of sociology, religion or morality. This readiness, accompanied by a true humility and deeply serious intent, I personally have encountered in nearly all 'other' Christians with whom it has fallen to me to discuss, especially in the various organs of the World Council. What a joy it is to feel that between oneself and another no barrier is interposed to prevent the practical acceptance of a truth however onerous it may be!

This can only be a living experience when it means a search for God himself, unconditional surrender to Jesus Christ, as a striving after holiness, by union with that which is the centre and source of all: the reality of Jesus Christ, as Lord and Saviour. This is why prayer, prayer by common intention and even, where possible, prayer together, constitutes the culminating point of ecumenical experience and activity. C. S. Lewis has finely said: 'The man who lives the Christian life most faithfully in his own Confession is spiritually nearest to those who are not under the same obedience. For the geography of the spiritual world is very different from that of the physical world. It is the lukewarm and indifferent in each region who are furthest away from every other country.'[1] If that is true, then one can understand that, devoting themselves utterly in obedience to such a call from God and in consecration to the Lord and Saviour Jesus Christ, those who take part in the ecumenical movement find, in this very participation, a way of sanctification and unification in their life which they cannot but feel to be blessed by God.

It is a way to conversion. It asks not less faith, but more. Ecumenism does not live by a purpose made up of doctrinal liberalism and of discarding, but of growth in a fuller and purer truth. And this it does by the hard road that encounters opposition from others, and leads to self-interrogation by each of us as we come face to face with our sources and with the truth. What have we ever yielded that should have been upheld? To whom have we ever yielded if not to the truth, which none has a right to resist, before which, on the contrary, it is such a joy to bend in obeisance. Ecumenism demands a profound moral and even religious conversion. But it is not for everyone to bring about, only the ecumenically minded: rather as a democracy can only be built by democrats, and fascism only introduced by fascists. It is a question of really reforming ourselves. As for me, who committed myself to the task thirty years ago, I reckon to have scarcely begun that reform and, like any Christian life, am destined to complete it only at my final passing to the life of light eternal.

One cannot but be greatly impressed by the life of Mahatma Gandhi, who although not a son of the Kingdom, so generously performed its duties and bore its fruits. Gandhi conceived his political work as involving purification of the heart and a real conversion, not only on his part and that of the leaders, but amongst the whole people. He who did his utmost to secure the independence of his country considered that India was not yet worthy of it, since it was still full of hatred and distrust.

[1] *The Problem of Pain*, Introduction to the French edition: Paris 1950, p. 28.

He wanted to achieve victory by conquering enmity: not only between Indians and British, but between Hindus and Moslems. Gandhi spent the last months of his life going from one Moslem village to another in peaceful and friendly fashion, saying: 'I have but one goal in sight and it is quite clear: the cleansing of the hearts of Hindus and Moslems by God, that these two groups may be freed from mutual suspicion and fear.' This cleansing of the heart was something Gandhi carried out within himself all his life, adapting his whole inner and even outward behaviour—whence his strange régime of nourishment—to his ideal of non-violence and love. What a lesson for us who know Jesus Christ!

Ecumenism seeks also a reform within ourselves, for we are full of agressiveness, clannishness and arrogance, of distrust and rivalry. We must be converted by detachment from all this and from ourselves, and acceptance of a humble submissiveness to what the Lord expects of us. One day he will judge all human history and the whole sociological aspect of the Christian world. Ecumenism is an effort to rediscover a unity amongst Christians in keeping at once with the unity of its beginnings in the Upper Room of the Last Supper and of Pentecost, and with that of its eschatological culmination. It seeks too, in the light of its origins and of eschatology, to anticipate the judgment that Christ will pass on the historical record of what has gone between.

Our Protestant brethren like to speak of repentance. So be it; provided that the word is divested of a certain possible tinge of romanticism. I should prefer to speak of conversion in relation to individuals, and of reform in relation to the Church. As to the conversion of individuals, there is no theological difficulty. Difficulties arise when it comes to the conversion (repentance) of the Church itself considered as such. Involvement in the ecumenical movement inevitably brings one up against the question of a penitence or repentance of the Church. And indeed, it is not on the surface that one encounters it, it is at the heart of the attitude taken up by many Christian brethren in response to the call they have heard. 'What was new in this ecumenical consciousness was that those who had it felt the judgment of God on the sin of schism addressed to *themselves*. They felt *themselves* called to repentance. The distinguishing feature of the ecumenical consciousness is that it is a consciousness of sin; the ecumenical movement is a movement of repentance.'[1]

It is always a problem for a Catholic to know to what extent, or rather on what grounds and in what sense, he can associate himself with such an attitude.[2] There certainly is a sense in which we can and do indeed do so; there is also a sense in which Catholics—and Orthodox—[3] are loth to speak of 'penitence', no less than they are of 'prevarication' or of 'sin' *of the Church*. This duality (not 'duplicity'!) of outlook itself shows that it is necessary to differentiate when one speaks of 'The Church'. The New Testament keeps for the word 'Church' its etymological meaning of convocation or assembly. But ideas have so evolved that Catholics often put in the first place, under this word, the transpersonal reality which corresponds, in human terms, to the covenant-relationships which God establishes in Jesus Christ. We would call it, in legal phraseology, the public institution established by divine right by Jesus Christ to mediate the salvation he offers us. If that is what one understands by 'Church', one cannot speak of sin, of schism, or of repentance in connection with it. It is, in fact, none other than the very institution of the Lord. Jesus is within it as its source ('*auctor*').

But one can also understand by 'Church' those who make up

[1] W. Nicholls, *Ecumenism and Catholicity*, SCM Press, London, 1952, p. 18f. Compare *Man's Disorder and God's Design* (Amsterdam Assembly of WCC) vol. II, *The Church's Witness to God's Design* (London 1948), p. 79; *Evanston Report*, First Section III (The Acts of Faith) para. 21.

[2] See my *Vraie et fausse réforme dans l'Eglise (Unam Sanctam 20)*, Paris, 1950; 'Comment l'Eglise sainte doit se renouveler sans cesse', in *Irénikon*, 34 (1961) p. 322-45 (and pamphlet); G. Dejaifve, 'Eglise catholique et Repentance oecuménique', in *Nouv. Rev. théol.*, 84 (1962) p. 225-39.

[3] See for example *Ecumenical Review*, Jan. 1952, p. 173.

God's People or Assembly: the ordinary congregation and the leaders (*praepositi*) who, having authority, represent or personify the *ecclesia*. It is in this sense that the New Testament and generally the Liturgy and the Fathers, use the word *ecclesia*. One could almost always translate it in their writings by 'the Christian community' or even 'the community of Christians'. The Church so understood is made up of men who are all sinners, who moreover have their limitations and bear a heavy load of physical, sociological, historical, ethnical and other factors that condition them. It is in them and through them that the institution itself takes on the concrete historical forms which define the form it originally received from our Lord and his Apostles. This collective entity is human and, by its very nature, limited and fallible. One cannot, however, attribute sins, in the strict and ethical sense of the word, to a collective subject, for, in this sense, sins can have as subjects only individual persons. But the responsible leaders—theologians, bishops and popes— commit sins in their sphere as responsible leaders, sins which, inasmuch as the leaders personify and represent the whole community, are considered without distinction as sins of the community. These same leaders and, to a lesser but nevertheless real extent, all the faithful, thus bear responsibility for bringing about certain situations in which the desire for improvement is not strong enough, in which mission, preaching, and doctrine are neglected, in which worldly postures of power and prestige are so highly developed, and shortcomings are so widely tolerated in worship, in the behaviour of the clergy, etc., that all this rouses the wrath of God and sometimes even the wrath of man.

We have in this way marked out a whole field—coextensive with the human history of the Church—which is the field of the Church's frailties, frailties for which all churchmen are responsible, and to some extent all the faithful, and for which the Church in the concrete and historic meaning of the word must indeed do penance.

In this respect the Catholic Church has always seemed to me very close to the elder son of whom the Gospel parable speaks (Matt. 21.28ff.): the one who says he will not go to the vineyard, but goes. The Catholic Church does not care much to speak about reform or to hear others speak about it, but it never ceases reforming itself, trying to conform more closely to the pattern of its Master and of his Apostles. In the end of the day, the differences between Catholics and Protestants are, in this field, at the same time less than is thought, and very great. Less, in that Catholic theology attributes infallibility and irreformability only to that which is in her of God (of Christ): in this respect, the Reformers do not speak differently. Very great, in that Catholic tradition admits the existence of a divine institution for salvation established in the world since the baptism of Jesus and since Pentecost as a public and visible institution, whereas Protestant theology seems to us to recognize as the sole agent of the work of salvation in individual persons, only Christ himself, as Lord most glorious, through his Holy Spirit. Catholic theology, on the other hand, acknowledges the visible Church as having truly received, through the foundation, promise and grace of the Lord, the attributes of indefectibility, and also the classic attributes of unity, sanctity, apostolicity, catholicity; whereas, if I am not mistaken, Protestant thought restricts these attributes either to Christ, or to the transcendent and invisible reality that we would rather call the Communion of saints.

Taking ecumenical experience and conversion, as I myself have known them, for my starting point, I have allowed myself to be carried away into *comparative Symbolics*, on a point which remains a very delicate one, desiring as I did to clarify it and to define the conditions of ecumenical conversion for a Catholic. The possibilities of such conversion remain immense: nothing less than the whole extent of the historical life of the Church. Eager to respond to the call and to the grace of ecumenism, we are faced today with the task of remedying what an accumulation of errors and misfortunes, omissions and inadvertencies, have rendered (if one may so phrase it) historically inevitable— the breach between East and West, and the dramatic religious division of the West, with all their consequences. The true penitence of the Church, that is to say of Christians, is not so much a matter of feelings and statements, as of the diligence with which that same Church is seeking today to act in such a way that, had it always so acted, it would have spared itself those two immense tragedies to which we have just alluded.

How much we shall need and how much has already been expended in the way of patience, true humility, the will to be faithful, endeavour, dedicated lives, suffering, prayer and entreaty, God knows. But what joy, for a Catholic heart filled with ecumenic passion, to see on all sides the seeds and plants flourishing and flowering that he has helped to water with his labours. '*Deus autem incrementum dedit*' (I Cor. 3.6). The return to biblical sources, the liturgical movement, the return to the Fathers, an active laity, mission, renewal of the Church's conciliar and community life, ecumenism: an upsurge! It is overwhelming, and sometimes one's eyes are filled with tears of love and thanksgiving. Yes, the hand of the Lord hath done this (Isa. 41.20). We can anticipate the universal thanksgiving which will fill the Heavens, and confess together: God has directed all and done all, 'Our sufficiency is of God' (II Cor. 3.5).

THE UNITY OF GRACE

Nikos A. Nissiotis

IT would be a great error if we were to support the idea that the intense work for restoring church unity is a main characteristic of our century only. Church history teaches us that there were always noble men who worked to bring separated churches together in all times and even immediately after the first schisms. But what is—perhaps!—new in our century—and this is, thanks to the men of the Ecumenical Movement, seen in the World Council of Churches and described as early as 1920 by the Encyclical of the Ecumenical Patriarchate of Constantinople—is the way in which the restoration of church unity is continuously in the path of realization. It is a life process of the churches—being together and staying together within a *koinonia* of life, a fellowship of a 'practical' nature, which conceals a deep understanding of the reality of the growing responsibility for sharing in the interchurch *diakonia*. It is only in this *situation* that the question of the nature of the unity we seek is posed afresh today and in a new way, that is in the *koinonia* of fellowship of the World Council of Churches, comprising faith and witness, confession and life, dogma and engagement of the churches together in this world. Therefore, we should no longer examine the dogmatic differences alone and seek to impose on the others any kind of consensus in matters of confession in order to reach a formula of agreement, unless we are first ready to share in the key work of God in Christ through the Holy Spirit to build up his community of newness of life beyond any kind of scholastic prescriptions which block the way to the biblical understanding of 'keeping the unity of the Spirit' (Eph. 4.3). This concept *in actu* of unity is far richer and more dynamic than all other definitions of unity that the human intellect, separated from the charismatic fountain of the Spirit of life in the Church, may suggest through the system of any school of thought. From the theological point of view the most interesting theme of our days, forced on us by the growing relationships of the churches, is the study of unity through the right understanding of the work of the Spirit to build up the community and the correct interpretation of the biblical *charisma*, the gift of grace of the same Spirit, as the constitutive power and element for maintaining church unity.

Grace and Gift of Grace

It is rather strange that theological discussion on grace has very often, in the history of theological thinking, been marked by confessional dispute between separated traditions. The result was that the theology taught in colleges and universities dealt more with the different interpretations of the effect of the grace of God in man, and centred the interest on the participation, the collaboration of man accepting this grace; or on the other hand with the question of the surplus of grace, or not, and the right of the Church, or not, to dispose of this grace as God's treasurer in this world. In this way the study of the nature of grace has been overshadowed by all these disputes. It is in modern times and to a great extent due to the event of the gathering together of different confessions, bringing as contribution to the restoration of Christian unity their charismatic life, that through the particular gift of grace, given by God to different people standing in different traditions, the fundamental question of grace can be posed anew to today's theology.

At the same time we owe a clear answer to today's laymen, standing on the border between the life of the Church and the life of the world, about what we mean when we speak of the grace of God realized in Christ Jesus. If we are allowed to attempt an approach to show the direction in which the inter-confessional discussion in an ecumenical setting should seek to find its way again in studying the most fundamental biblical term of the Christian faith, we would say that the grace is the power which flows out of the act of redemption in Christ in order to restore man through the Holy Spirit to his original position, that is to say to communion with God.

It is difficult to understand now what this communion with the trinitarian God is, but this very meeting of the different church traditions makes us realize more and more that the gifts of grace reflect this communion as an historical event which has already taken place in this world in a visible form in the concrete fellowship of all of us in the One Body. The echo of the incomprehensible grace of God is clearly heard only in his earthly community. 'God is faithful, by whom ye are called unto the fellowship of his Son Jesus Christ our Lord' (I Cor. 1.9). It is a fellowship of the biblical *koinonia* and exists as grace in movement and action, both for the restored communion with God in Christ and for the immediate reality of the earthly community, the other *koinonia* that we have in his Body, our community of believers, 'as thou, Father, art in me, and I in thee, that they also may be one in us' (John 17.21). We have here both things; first the restoration of communion with God in Christ, and second our belonging together as an inseparable whole, a community which reflects the power of the grace realized in Christ; therefore, only when we come together and live together in the One Body, do we dispose of the reality of grace and the possibility of returning again and again and remaining within the fulness of belonging together with God.

In this sense we must recapture as separate traditions the

power to reaffirm that this fellowship with God of which the Bible speaks is not a category for philosophizing or theologizing in a formal way. It is not a simple principle of life or of thinking, or a moral code for social life. This communion is the immediacy of God's presence in time with us saved men as concrete historical unbroken fellowship. Therefore, communion with God is to be understood only through and in the established communion of God amongst men. St John who like an eagle, in the prologue to his gospel, flies over the earth with a celestial vision gained through the incarnation and resurrection of Christ, alights on the earth and brings this whole vision into the immediate reality of our life together as One Body and on this earth. 'If a man say, I love God, and hateth his brother, he is a liar' (I John 4.20). Every vision and theory about the restored communion of men with God is judged and decided in the historical fellowship of his Body. The theological problem of the communion as grace realized is for us the every-day problem of an ecclesiological and anthropological nature; it is the axis of the whole creation, the centre of history, namely the unbroken community of believers. In this we are invisibly fitted together . . . there we have to live; there is the fact that we have to accept—this community which does not derive from our agreement on what we understand of grace, but from the reality of receiving it through his One Body on the condition that we remain there. We must make it clear again and again in our minds that this is his community; it is what he has done in order that we might have immediate access to the tremendous event of the restoration of our communion with God. It deprives us of understanding in an intellectual way what is happening, but it gives to us his reality as a new life.

The nature of grace is not to be identified with the result of grace, justification by faith; neither with a surplus of grace and the rights of the Church deriving from this quantitative understanding of what God has done for us. The nature of grace is the once-and-for-all gathered communion of saints and believers to live, with all those who are saved through faith, with God. The matter is, therefore, more how to grow in this community, how to keep this community a real and unbroken one. The grace of God is not a simple discussion of the justification of man but it points the road back to God by fitting us together in his family. God never obliges us by grace; he does not give a gift like a king or a tyrant, but he liberates men from themselves and their isolation and invites them back, having given already the immediate means of achieving this.

The trinitarian God of the Christian faith is not the isolated 'it' but a personal will; that is to say a God who is always coming to meet and create a gathering in his name. The doctrine of the Trinity tries precisely to express what is the life-process that comes to meet us and create a communion of persons which defeats equally individualism and collectivism. This process should never be thought of as a set form which governs the life of the group. The grace of the Christian God does not seem to be of this kind in the Bible. We can never possess with absolute certainty the reality in which he has fitted us together; there are moments of solidarity and moments of alienation; there is a struggle, a falling away from his will and a coming back to it. But what affords the community of God its unshaken basis is the transcending power of his grace, seen in the fruits of the Holy Spirit; that is to say the manifold expression of his person is through the gifts of grace. That is why the Bible teaches so very clearly that the incarnation and redemption imply that God abides here amongst us in his *Ecclesia;* his communion with man is this communion that we have in the *Ecclesia.* Everything in the life of the Church has to be continuously restored and renewed, but only in and through this *Ecclesia,* or else it has no sense at all. The People of God is his community here and now: it is this affirmation that the Bible makes by pointing continually to the close relationship between the Head and the Body and the consistent functions of the members fitted into it.

The Unity of Grace

The House of God as a Building

This idea of the community as a given and accomplished reality in time and yet as a process of becoming and growing is expressed in the Bible in an outstanding way by the idea of the building, *oikodome*. The biblical *oikodome* bears both aspects described above—a solid basis and a continuing process of building. The building is not an entirely finished house; it stands here bearing all the necessary elements for habitation, but men are not yet entirely equipped to live in it. God's act of giving does not overcome by his grace man's limited ability to receive. To explain these words especially to Evangelicals, I must say that we do not mean that the gift of grace is conditioned by man, but rather we take into serious consideration the sinfulness of man, received into the holiness of God's building. The paramount importance of grace is precisely that man's revolt against God's holy will *is unable to affect the building of God*. On the other hand, it affirms that the grace of God cannot operate as an automatic machine. It is given for salvation in a complete way; therefore, it points to a new freedom of man to abide in God's house and to share in the restoration of his community. Here the grace of God can be given in vain if we fail to share with God the immense responsibility of maintaining his building and abide in it as one community growing together through his gifts of grace. It is in this way that we can understand the words of St Paul, 'We then, as workers together with him, beseech you also that ye receive not the grace of God in vain' (II Cor. 6.1). It is the tragic refrain of the Christian faith that one can receive the grace of God in vain, a fact that has nothing to do with the fulness of grace but with man's failure to respond. The question is how we can be certain that we have received the grace not in vain. The answer in the Bible seems to me to be clear, in so far as the grace for remaining in the community is seen always as an operation of the *charismata* of the Holy Spirit. We can, therefore, say that the grace is not given to us in vain when it is used for the edification of the communion of saints, as a contribution for preserving and permitting a close link between the members of the one unbroken Body.

It is in this way that the building of God in the Bible is continuously being perfected. This scandalous phrase that the Body of Christ, already given and established, has still to be built further by men means that being a member of the Church one has to become a true member and justify his membership by offering his particular gift of grace, not in order to provide for the Body, not as an exceptional power, not as a revolutionary uprising, but as a responsibility given by God in order to maintain the solidarity of the members throughout the whole world.

The Building into which we have to be built together

We can, therefore, say that the gift of grace—*charisma*—is the grace in action given in a personal way, namely that one member contributes through it to building further the community. The *charisma* is the existential expression of *charis*; it is the vessel of grace, grace shown forth in action. The right use of the gift of God deriving from Christ's redemption is to maintain and edify, with the other members, the One Body. 'As every man hath received the gift, even so minister the same one to another, as good stewards of the manifold grace of God' (I Peter 4.10).

The answer to the big question of what maintains the unity of this Body should never remain in the abstract form either of a verbal confession or of a global but docetic statement, such as, 'Christ himself the Head of the Body maintains it.' The Bible presents us with an existential struggle which begins when the Head transmits to the Body concrete tasks, in whose fulfilment the Body is quickened. These are the gifts of grace, the manifold *charismata*, which once put into operation amongst us by the Holy Spirit can be recognized as authentic only if they are used as dynamic connections, binding the members together in the One Body. No single operation of any gift of grace can be exempted from this truth, according to the biblical text. When making an act of simple thanksgiving to God the individual who has received the gift must seek to express it in a corporate way. In, through and for the community all *charismata* are tested as true or not, and every act of every believer has to be judged as truly done in the Name of Christ and through the power of the Holy Spirit. Corporate, communal thanksgiving seems to be in the Bible the seal of the authenticity of a personal gift of God given to an individual, because it reminds us simply that all gifts are given to one person but in, through and for the whole Body, the one unbroken community. 'Ye also helping together by prayer for us, that for the gift bestowed upon us by the means of many persons thanks may be given by many on our behalf' (II Cor. 1.11).

The gift of grace is received only in the community. The *charisma* at first intensifies our personal life of faith; out of a confession ever new action springs in a particular situation, thus contributing to the maintenance and growth of the same community. This means that to face the danger of generalizing and accepting superficially every apparently good action of an individual, the Bible gives us the criterion for discerning the true *charismata* from the false and distinguishing between the gifts of grace received in the Body of Christ and for co-edification in it, and the gifts of grace received by all men within the creation of the One God and Creator of all. This criterion is precisely the work of the building up of the house which is already built for us 'upon the foundation of the Apostles and Prophets, Jesus Christ himself being the chief corner stone' (Eph. 2.20).

This is the fundamental truth of the operation of the *charismata*. Only on this basis can we understand and maintain the infinite diversity of the gifts of grace and regard them all as indispensable, though so different one from another, for the building of the community. It is on this basis that the second chapter of the Epistle to the Ephesians presupposes the act of God implanting us, fitting us into the already existing building prepared by him for us. But this building is not made of stones which remain passively where they have been placed. It is becoming an active body and the living stones are endowed with new life through the gifts of grace, only if they live, move and work together in a close interdependence. That is why St Paul, after he has spoken of this first act of God fitting and framing us together, speaks of us in this building of the Lord, where we are builded together. It is very significant that, for the first act of God, St Paul has used the passive form with the preposition 'upon'—*epi*—saying that we have been built upon the foundation—*epoikodomethentes*—but for the second he uses the middle form of the verb with the preposition *syn*, 'ye are builded together'—*synoikodomeisthe* (2.22). The text shows us clearly that the first act of God leads inevitably to the second. The passive form of the first verb does not signify that man remains passive, but that God acts; the second verb again does not mean that man acts, because the form is middle, but that man acts only through the grace received from God by being built together upon the foundation, and only together with the other members, in and for the community. It is only in this way that man reaches the supreme purpose of his redemption in Christ, namely to become 'an habitation of God through the Spirit' (2.22) and thus by being built together in God's *oikodome* he becomes his own building: 'Ye are God's building' (1 Cor. 3.9).

Here we must take careful note, because this biblical verse has often been subjected to two extremist interpretations. To become God's habitation through the Spirit means very often, for some totally devoted members of the Church, a kind of exclusive and 'individual—churchly' experience which leads them to neglect the communal and missionary aspect of the charismatic life. On the other hand this strong affirmation of the Bible, that God is always working to make his people his habitation through the Spirit, combined with the cosmic, universal meaning of Christ's redemptive act on the cross, has led many in our days to regard many of man's actions in daily life and in the secular realm as charismatic, almost in the same sense as those actions that the Bible describes as constitutive charismatic elements for the building up of the Body of Christ (as described in texts such as I Cor. 12, Rom. 12.6ff., etc.). The first extremist attitude seeks to isolate the Christian from the world and introduces a rigid separation of the House of God—his building—from the cosmos, his creation redeemed and restored in Christ. The second attitude generalizes the *charisma*, seeing it as spread throughout the whole world, without necessarily the personal commitment in the Church through faith, and the fundamental gift of grace springing up from the act of being fitted into the Body of Christ through Baptism and participation in the Eucharist. The first separates the Church from the world; the second identifies her with it.

Both of these attitudes find their point of departure in the Bible and are to a certain extent justified exaggerations, but only in a rigid and single direction. They represent easy and enthusiastic exaggerations, while the biblical text does not allow of such simple and monolithic interpretations. We must notice that the *charismata* in the Bible are not so simply and exclusively, ecclesiastically and sacramentally bound, but on the other hand they are never entirely set free from the Church to become merely worldly phenomena on the basis of a vague, cosmic and general salvation given to all men in Christ. The charismatic texts of the Bible should never lead us, either to a false separation between Church and world, or to a superficial identification of the one with the other. We should never oppose sacramental to profane, but rather distinguish between sacred and secular.

On the basis of this distinction the sacramental grace is the fountain of the gifts of grace. These *charismata* are not given to us in order to enclose us in the Body as saved members; but in order that we might through them look at the gifts of grace scattered throughout the whole world as given also by God the Creator to all men. We must, in other words, distinguish these *charismata* which edify the church community from the others which operate in the world and are also under the Lordship of the same Lord of the Church and of the world. The whole creation exists and is preserved by God the Creator and all cultural, scientific and economic developments are possible only thanks to the manifold grace of God. But these *charismata* are still natural talents, certainly God-given but not yet used to the full, not Christ's gifts to the members of his Body, that is, they are not yet ecclesiastical.

This distinction—and not separation!—has a very great importance for the activity of the churches in the modern world and for their concern for promoting church reunion. It signifies that the churches, on the one hand, have an inner charismatic life, but, on the other hand, this life cannot remain an internal ecclesiastical affair. Through the inner charismatic life the historical churches, liberated from their sectarian and parochial vision of the world, look for and recognize the gifts of grace of the One Lord also in the world outside the Church, yet not in the same way as the *charismata* within the Church. The 'outside' *charismata* are an invitation to those inside the Church to act together in order to use fully these gifts outside the Church, because those inside are vehicles of the power of the Holy Spirit to manifest the Lordship of Christ in the world. They are signposts pointing to the restoration and recapitulation of the whole creation, and they are still to be incorporated into the One Body of Christ, which is the *Ecclesia*. We should not confuse the *charismata* given for the maintenance of the unity of the Body with those given to the world. The purpose of this distinction is precisely to enable us to understand in the right way and act accordingly in the world as one Church, equipped by the Spirit with the manifold gifts of grace given to the historical churches.

The diversity of the gifts of grace exists within the church community so that it may keep its unity and at the same time turn to the outside world and use fully the 'outside' *charismata* that God has given to be a point of contact between Church and world. Everyone outside the Church lives by virtue of a specific *charisma* of God. That is why all can receive Christ as him who fulfils all in all, by using fully the life-bearing *charisma* given to them by the grace which flows from the church communion. The *charis*, the grace of God, always springs up from within the *Ecclesia* to the outside world through the diversity of the *charismata* with which it endows the members of the church community. There is maintained therefore, on the basis of the distinction between sacred and profane, a contact, better an existential continuity, shown as solidarity between Church and world by the threefold operation of the diversity of the gifts of grace in the Church; this operation is the *receiving* of the grace in the One Body, the *maintaining* through the gifts of grace of the unity of this Body and the *extending* of this unity to the secular realm, using fully the *charismata*, given to the world as vessels of this grace.

That is why only the faithful, living within the charismatic ecclesiastical community, engaged in missionary activity today in this period of universal history and in the modern technological age, can understand the meaning of the triumphant words of the Bible, '. . . by him all things consist. And he is the head of the body, the church' (Col. 1.17-18). The vision of the restored creation (*ktisis*) belongs only to the consciously faithful church member; and not to the man living in a selfish isolation owing to his strong conception of sacramental grace as saving once and for all; nor to the 'incognito' non-ecclesiastically bound 'Christian' in the realm of secular life, simply serving the world through his talent as artist, poet, physician, etc. Both are deprived of this vision by their non-communal use of *charisma*, received in the Church for the whole cosmos and summed up in the same One Church. God, after the redemptive act of Christ and his resurrection and by his Spirit, penetrates and fills the whole world by the gifts of grace which flow out of his Body, the *Ecclesia*. The movement is always from within the Church to the outside world and not *vice versa*. 'But unto every one of us is given grace according to the measure of the gift of Christ . . . that he might fill all things' (Eph. 4.7, 10).

We should never confuse the order which preserves the fallen creation of God, with the charismatic ecclesiastical community. The natural order, after Christ's redemption, has to pass through the personal commitment of faith, the incorporation in the One Body through Baptism and thus become the charismatic church community. It is only in this way that the Bible, through the diversity of the *charismata* of the Spirit in the One Church, speaks of a direct Lordship of Christ within his building, and through it points out the indirect one yet to be achieved through the mission of the charismatic Church in the whole world. There is, therefore, no separation between the two aspects of the gifts of grace, but we must make a clear distinction for the missionary purposes of the historical churches acting together in the world. This distinction prepares for permanent solidarity maintained by the charismatic nature of the *Ecclesia* flowing out to the world by a charismatic mission in which all the historical churches are engaged together.

The Charismatic Community within the Church of Unity

The diversity of gifts of grace is given precisely for the maintenance of the unity of the Christian community within a changing world and for church mission, diverse in forms and methods, still one, yet appropriate to different times and world situations. The clash, therefore, between those who have received the gifts of grace is an immediate sign of the sinfulness of man and his desire to keep individually all that he possesses, introducing separation instead of working further for the spiritual equipment of the charismatic community. The great danger arises where anyone, on the basis of his *charisma*, thinks of himself more highly than he ought to think, not respecting the measure of faith that God has assigned to him by giving him a special *charisma* (Rom. 12.3). St Paul shows how this threatens to split the charismatic community as a devilish spirit. The Christian is always tempted—for the sake of defending truth and right action!—to abuse his God-given *charisma*. In the twelfth chapter of his Epistle to the Romans, St Paul speaks of the charismatic community after giving them a severe warning, trying to restrain them from any kind of selfish and individualistic use of their *charismata*. The gifts of grace have meaning—as we have several times remarked above—only if and when, put into operation by the Spirit, they become means for binding the members together, strengthening and nourishing the community as one unbroken spiritual family.

An objection can be made here; namely that we sacrifice truth and new developments in the church community simply for the sake of unity. This problem is extremely complex; we admit it. However, one should not interpret our words as referring only to those, who for the sake of truth 'depart' from an established and hierarchical church community causing a split in it, but equally to those responsible leaders and members of the community, who fail to use and incorporate a new *charisma*, which at first seems to be revolutionary! The problem that we face here is very delicate and no easy answer can be given because a *charisma* does not seem to have always, solely and automatically, a good and positive effect on the community. When God gives, he never uses man as a machine, but he invites him to a hard effort of sacrifice and humility, whether he is a church leader, bearer of the charismatic order of sacerdotal leadership in an organized church community, or a simple charismatic church worker who wants to lead the church people to new ways of interpretation of the Bible or of mission and evangelism. It is, therefore, imperative that, in this difficult question, we try to find the solution in every particular case and avoid general conclusions. Church history tells us of a dramatic clash between the charismatic hierarchical order and the charismatic persons; in many cases we cannot say where the responsibility lies for the sad event of church division and the answer is not very easy for us. If we attempt to draw general conclusions from the biblical text and in the light of church history and the ecumenical relationships of today, the only thing we can say is that every *charisma* given to every member of the Church must be accepted and practised as a gift of grace which flows out from the redemptive sacrifice of the blood of Jesus on the cross. This signifies that every charismatic person cannot be simply and automatically truly charismatic unless he sees his *charisma* through the self-humiliation of Jesus (Phil. 2.5-8). The kenotic understanding of the gift of grace belongs to its essence and forms its backbone. Sacrifice is the charismatic essence of the Christian life *par excellence*. Therefore, to be truly charismatic and edify the community through a special *charisma*, means a period of suffering, of self-denial, of temptation and above all of patience till one makes faithful use of one's *charisma* in the community. God, in his mercy and precisely for the sake of the charismatic person, does not always allow the fruits of a *charisma* to be seen immediately during the short period of a lifetime.

It is from this angle and after a thorough and deep study of the biblical understanding of the charismatic life of a church community that the churches in ecumenical relationships have to look back again and again at church history to try to find the deeper causes of the church schisms. It can be that there are schisms which are to a certain extent results of individual 'apostasies'; there are other schisms that clearly show us today that a *charisma* was wrongly rejected or scorned and unjustifiably condemned by the official leadership of the church community.

Accordingly, one could say that in every schism there is a dangerous, risky and delicate moment of decision, which reveals the immense responsibility of the charismatic person, applying his *charisma* to the service of his church or of the world. We should never forget, and let us repeat it, that on the basis of a gift of grace a charismatic person cannot operate as a robot or as an automatic machine always producing good results in the hard work of building the community. If the *charismata* were like this, to keep church unity would be a very easy affair, for it would be a God-given, God-maintained and God-promoted solid unity.

It is evident that a study of the process of building up through the gifts of grace the already-built church community is of primary importance if we are to enter into an effective discussion of the problem of church unity today. Without a careful study of the charismatic community, its nature and function and particularly without sharing existentially in prayer, study and action, in a charismatic community composed of members of different church traditions, no fruitful encounter on the problem of unity is possible.

Especially for Eastern Orthodoxy, which has always maintained its unity as charismatic and through an ever-renewed decision of all charismatic persons to submit freely to the charismatic order expressed by the consciousness of the whole Church, laity and clergy, this life together with the 'others' and the careful study of the function of the *charisma* seems to be the necessary prelude to the theme of church unity. Eastern Orthodoxy witnesses to just this, that in every schism there is a heavy ethical responsibility on both sides. The choice of a new direction in church life and theology is possible only within the one unbroken Church; no *charisma*, if it is a true *charisma* applied in the true biblical way, should ever cause a split in the Body of Christ from which it springs.

What do these words really mean? Do they imply a pious fatalism or a false passivity incompatible with the evangelical *kerygma* of a continually renewed missionary action in the contemporary world? It can appear so to an activist who sees the Church solely and always in pilgrimage in this world, without inner life and unshaken coherence as One Body by the grace of God to live in unbroken continuity by means of specific church actions and by the submission of the individual to an already framed pattern of life, faith and thought. But for an Eastern Orthodox this unbroken historical continuity, namely the respect for the unbroken and pre-existing unity prescribed and maintained by the 'inner' charismatic life of the Church as such, is the one and indispensable condition both for building up the Christian community and for acting as One Church in the world of today. Certainly, it is through the charismatic life of separated Christians living together that we can recapture the vision of the unity of the whole Church; it seems so today in the abnormal situation of church division. Yet the careful study of charismatic life in the Bible reveals to us the fundamental truth that the churches do not create their unity. The very concept of 'Church' is nonsensical except as the Church *of* the charismatic unity, which God establishes, pouring out his grace upon his chosen people on the Day of Pentecost through the Holy Spirit, and which is based on Christ's sacrifice and resurrection. Without faith in this pre-existing charismatic unity which binds all together, no vision of the One Church, through the gifts of grace and common action of the churches today, is possible; for the foundation of the Church is coincident with the establishment of the Oneness of the Church. The *charis* of God, through his trinitarian energy, binds God and all men who believe in Christ in one family. The gifts of grace consequently do not only create unity but before this they spring up from the union of God with men; therefore, they are *charismata* which come from the pre-existing charismatic unity of God in his Church. The current expression, 'the unity of the Church we seek', has to be understood as referring to the Church of the already given charismatic unity. Because a church community cannot exist unless it is the outcome of grace, redeeming and uniting, and through this unity edifying further the community through the gifts of grace of the Holy Spirit.

The gifts of grace which bind the church members together in their life in the One Body and in their action together for the world are visible reminders to us of the Church of the charismatic unity. In other words the whole difficult operation of the gifts of grace in an ecumenical era such as ours should point out to us the first essential of our being and belonging together to the charismatic oneness given by God as corporate life; through it we are framed together in his own building. This means that before the expression of unity through confessions of faith must come its origin and the continuous activity of maintaining and promoting unity through life, which we call tradition; whose echo we find in the Scriptures and whose power we receive through the manifold *charismata* of the Spirit, which form all believers into one family. Unity and union precede and prescribe our whole charismatic life, because the *charismata* are possible only as results of and only in this unity flowing out in charismatic life and action. 'The Church of the charismatic unity' means that our whole being and action as church members are utterly dependent on the uniting grace of God; it is the grace which in Christ constitutes and nourishes the churches through the Spirit by specific gifts of grace.

It is in this way that we have to understand the paradox of being framed together in the one building of God on the foundation of the Apostles and Prophets and, on this basis, still having to be further built together till we become a habitation of God through the Spirit. We understand thus why we have to make the fine distinction between the *charismata* within the Church and the *charismata* given to the world and to avoid all kinds of generalizations. Without this distinction the fourth chapter of the Epistle to the Ephesians might seem to those struggling honestly for restoring unity a riddle presenting a dilemma, or rather a dualism. But on the contrary once the distinction has been carefully made, this text shows clearly how the members are fitted together in the One Body. There is not a word in this chapter about creating or seeking or restoring unity through the *charismata*, but about keeping the unity of the Spirit (v.3) and growing into the perfect unity of faith (v.13) through the *charismata* which are given for the edifying of the Body of Christ. All this is possible only if and because we are called in one hope, having one faith and being baptized in the one baptism (v.5). These acts are not to be regarded either as confessionalistic or as magical but as the indispensable and distinctive charismatic source, within the Church, of all other gifts of grace, the *sine qua non* beginning of the long and difficult process of dynamic charismatic life which has to follow; this life is possible only when the local churches try to maintain the unity by the gifts of grace, through their charismatic members acting together with a universal vision of the catholic Church; for their *charismata* are given to them only after those fundamental acts of being incorporated together into the One Body of the whole *Ecclesia*.

The incorporation is given through baptism which is the source of all *charismata*, but the charismatic life in the one *Ecclesia* is the growth in faith and the confirmation of this faith by a life continually renewed through the *charismata* of the Holy Spirit. That is why the Eastern churches regard only as the first step the threefold baptismal immersion as symbolizing the death with Jesus, and the rising from the waters as symbolizing the resurrection with him into a newness of life (according to Rom. 6.4). But this 'newness of life' is given by the Church as a charismatic gift of the Holy Spirit through the second phase of the baptism which is seen in the Eastern traditions as of equal importance with the first, namely the 'chrismation' through the Holy *Myron* (chrism) according to biblical texts, such as 'in whom also after that ye believed, ye

were sealed with that holy Spirit of promise' (Eph. 1.13). (See
also Eph. 4.30; II Cor. 1.22.) The incorporation of the faithful
through baptism becomes then dynamic sharing in the gifts of
grace of the Spirit, which manifests and maintains the pre-
existing unity of the Body. The chrismation as 'sealing' has a
double meaning: it is first the grace which strengthens and
endows the baptized person with the newness of life in the
One Body, and second it is the certain and glorious manifestation that the faithful baptized is once and for all numbered
among the members of the unbroken and undivided Church
of the charismatic unity. The Holy Spirit as Giver of life and
treasurer of all good things binds all into the one family, where
alone the charismatic unity can be maintained and his
charismata can be practised as binding connections and inseparable links between the 'sealed' members. Without this act
the whole of the charismatic life loses the genuine ecclesiastical
basis directly related to the act of incorporating a new member
into the Body through baptism. When we speak of baptism, we
must recapture this old act of the charismatic unity for all
historical churches engaged in a charismatic community life
through the ecumenical movement. It is then that we could
together face the difficult problem of re-articulating our faith
in the One Church, if this proves to be necessary, and speak
again of communion from the one eucharistic cup without
using the scandalous word 'intercommunion', which betrays
a noble desire to restore unity but in an abnormal situation. For
in the One Church of the charismatic unity there must be only
One Communion which is not simply the means to restore
unity but that which *par excellence* nourishes and maintains the
pre-existing charismatic unity of the 'together-and-through-
one-*myron*-sealed' faithful in and through the One Universal
Church. We are not yet mature enough in our ecumenism to
work out the practical details of the restoration of this fundamental act for all churches throughout the whole world, as the
churches might decide to apply it anew as the beginning of the

end of their ecumenical, charismatic movement in the Spirit.

The great thing is that this question is going to be raised from within the churches in their ecumenical relationships, because they are already sharing charismatically their God-given fellowship. They grow, as potentially full members one with another, towards their unique source which is at the same time their unique goal. That is why, as was said above, the ecumenism of our days approaches the old problem of restoring unity in a way different from past generations. This way can be described as passing through prayer, study and life together as well as through missionary and evangelistic action together. That is, without being sealed in the same Spirit by and in the One *Ecclesia*, the church members of the divided traditions are called upon by the Spirit to see the infinite dimensions of their pre-existing charismatic unity; to see, beyond theories, agreements and disagreements in the restoration of unity, the charismatic *praxis*. Though this *praxis* is not immediately manifest in the churches as they lack the concrete charismatic act of the common concrete beginning within the One Body, they are, nevertheless, converging upon their common origin, namely their charismatic unity, which alone articulates the faith and faces the problem of keeping the unity.

Today's ecumenism as charismatic, therefore, places at the centre of our enterprise, and rightly so, the problem of communion in the One Church (and not intercommunion between churches). The *charis* to sustain us in the One Body is given in and through the eucharistic fellowship both as the beginning and the crowning event of a consistent ecumenical, charismatic dialogue, and as the sole necessary condition for the exchange of all other *charismata* among the separated traditions in worship, preaching, evangelism, mission and inter-church *diakonia*. Without any revolutionary act it seems that the young ecumenical generation is on the right charismatic road to restoring the One Communion in the Body and Blood of Jesus, not as a show of unity for ecumenical propaganda but as the expression of the pre-existing charismatic unity, which holds the churches together in ecumenical discussion and action. It is precisely through their intense preoccupation with building together the Body of Christ as active members of this One Body that the Church is appearing afresh to the minds, eyes and faith of this generation as the One *Ecclesia* of the charismatic unity. It is by building the community that the Church of charismatic unity becomes a reality, a conquering power which demands the sacrifice of all kinds of individualism and self-sufficiency and poses the problem of the one eucharistic communion for all who recognize their common charismatic origin, being sealed in the One Church. They prepare themselves for common missionary and evangelistic action as members of the One Body, continuing to build the community and acting together through the diversity of the gifts of grace, the *charismata*, that they can receive only in the One Building of God.

Only in this way can the ecumenical movement be a sincere and pure effort in the sight of God and meaningful in and for today's world. For it is a movement of *charismata* for the sake of action together by all believers of different traditions, 'for the perfecting of the saints, for the work of the ministry, for the edifying of the body of Christ' (Eph. 4.12). This is the unseen goal of today's ecumenical charismatic intercourse which does not immediately raise the problem of the restoration of confessional unity but which silently poses it through the charismatic inter-church fellowship within the one unbroken *koinonia*. This is the path in which the Spirit leads the churches in our time, without allowing their members any superficial optimism, any emotional and enthusiastic naïveté, any revolutionary act. The idea of unity, which each tradition conceives, springs now from the work they do together in the One Church and for the whole world. No docetic, formalistic concept of unity is possible any more; but a conscious life of the churches together, a life consistent with the charismatic nature of their pre-existing and God-given unity. Ecumenism consists in trying to express this kind of charismatic unity by a common faith and common evangelism and mission in today's world, thus believing, praying and acting in close interdependence bound together through their mutual liturgical, evangelistic and missionary *diakonia*.

THE DEVELOPMENT OF A SOCIAL ETHIC IN THE ECUMENICAL MOVEMENT

Reinhold Niebuhr

I T is one of Visser 't Hooft's many creative contributions to the ecumenical movement, for which he has furnished such brilliant leadership for almost half a century (if the prelude in the Student Christian Movement is counted, as it must be) that he has always insisted that a closer and more creative encounter between the various non-Roman churches must be based upon, and must result in, the renewal of the churches. Without this presupposition and consequence the ecumenical movement will merely result in added ecclesiastical machinery.

In no department of the World Council's activities is this creative renewal of the churches more apparent than in the field of gradually elaborating a Christian social ethic, which would express the spirit of the Gospel on the one hand and be relevant on the other hand to the ever increasing complexities of a technical civilization and a budding world community, riven by a 'cold war' and living under the shadow of a nuclear catastrophe.

This task is, and was, an enormous one. It is so enormous because the New Testament has only the barest suggestions of a social ethic with its 'nicely calculated less and more.' The ethic of the New Testament is eschatological and ultimate. The Sermon on the Mount, which nineteenth-century liberalism regarded as a fount of the 'Social Gospel', represents ethics in the *n*th degree. Professor Dodd rightly declares that it suggests the 'quality and the direction of our ethical motives' rather than detailed and practical prescriptions for action in situations in which it is necessary to arbitrate between conflicting and competing claims. Jesus, in answer to the man who implored him 'Tell my brother to divide his inheritance with me', replied rather gruffly 'Who has made me a divider between you?' The emphasis in the answer deals with the attitudes which cause strife between the brothers and not with the substantive problems of justice by which conflicting claims are adjudicated. This encounter presents in a nutshell the problem of relating a social ethic to, or deriving it from, the spirit of the gospel.

The ethic of the synoptic gospels is eschatological in its framework and in substance enjoins the purest love. The *agape* of the New Testament is expressed in the Sermon on the Mount or in St Paul's hymn of love in I Corinthians 13, in which the apostle goes so far as to distinguish *agape* from the most rigorous actions of self-denial: 'Though I give all my goods to feed the poor—though I give my body to be burned, and have not love, it profiteth me nothing'. *Agape* represents a motive so pure that no seemingly sacrificial action can guarantee its expression. We are dealing, in short, with the pinnacles of the moral and spiritual life in the pages of the New Testament and not with the stresses and strains of a community of self-seeking men. The ideal community, the body of Christ, is compared with the body in which the members are 'fitly joined together', in which they are admonished to 'bear one another's burdens' and 'If one member suffer all members suffer with it' (I Cor. 12). In short, self-sacrificing love is rightly regarded as the mainspring of mutual love. *Agape* is transmuted into *philia*. But only in an ideal family or an ideal Christian community is this mutuality attained. The real problem of a social ethic is how to make justice, with its calculations of rights, the instrument of love, that is of the primal love commandment which enjoins us to be responsible for our neighbour.

If an ethic were drawn merely from these eschatological heights without any recognition that there is 'a law in my members which wars against the law that is in my mind' as Paul confesses (Romans 7) Christianity would be no more than a system of rigorous moral idealism, prescribing responsibilities which are on the very edge of historical possibilities. It was the error of nineteenth-century liberalism to reduce Christianity to this dimension.

But the Christian faith is not simply a rigorous idealistic system after the manner of Stoicism. It searches the heart and discovers the tragic antinomy between the law of love, which Paul calls the 'law of God' in which he delights 'after the inward man' and the law in his members which is obviously the law of self-love. The whole New Testament *kerygma* presupposes a basic variance between human desires and ambitions and the divine will, for which the atoning death of Christ is the answer in terms of forgiveness and new life. Christ is not a noble martyr, dying for his ideals but a revelation of the divine mercy: 'God was in Christ reconciling the world unto himself.' The New Testament *kerygma* is soteriological, dealing with the ultimate possibilities of human existence and with the tragic contradictions in the human heart. The problem of a Christian social ethic is how to profit from both the heights of its idealism and the depth of its realism in constructing systems of order and justice which provide for a tolerable harmony in communities of selfish men, who may or may not be touched by the divine law, 'written into their hearts'.

We cannot come to terms with the problem of a non-Roman Christian social ethic if we do not take the comparative adequacy and final inadequacy of the whole system of social morality of the Catholic church into consideration. Beginning

The Sufficiency of God

with Origen, Catholicism borrowed, first from Stoic and finally from Aristotelian, but always from classical, metaphysical sources, its elements of a social ethic. Classical metaphysical foundations were bound to betray it into the consideration of too fixed norms of 'natural law' in which the endless contingencies of history were obscured. Thus Catholicism, particularly through the Thomistic borrowings from Aristotle, was able to adjust the norms of the natural law to the ideologies of medieval feudalism and to obscure the rigours of the earlier Stoicism, which had attracted Chrysostom and Augustine and made the Greek fathers so radical.

Roman Catholicism, by reason of equating the historically contingent standards of feudalism with the ultimate norms of the natural law, has proved itself incapable of giving radical criticism to the feudal structures or extricating itself from the medieval-feudal mould of community. But this great weakness plus its incredible fixed position on birth control in a neo-Malthusian age must not obscure its very considerable achievements in relating its life to, and guiding the conscience of, modern technical society, once the radical emancipation has been accomplished with the help of others. The obvious reason for this accomplishment is that it has never questioned the social substance of human existence. It always knew that a tolerable harmony in the community would have to avail itself of calculations of justice, though it may have underestimated the ideological distortions in its own conceptions of justice.

If anyone should question the reality of this achievement, one need only to cite the fact that the Catholic church never lost the loyalty of the industrial workers in Western Europe to the same extent as Protestantism. The social and political realities in Belgium, Holland, Germany and America reveal the point.

The Reformation naturally had a greater emphasis on the realities of grace, and resisted the tendency to make love into a more rigorous law, which only the ascetic 'first class' Christians could keep. It rightly regarded love as the fruit of grace, which was universally available. But we must not assume that the Reformation soteriology and doctrines of grace automatically made for an adequate social ethic, which must deal with that peculiar mixture of grace and sin embodied in any system of justice. A system of justice is a realm of sin because only a tolerable equilibrium of power will prevent sinful men from taking advantage of each other. It is a realm of common grace because only given and traditional modes of mutuality, beyond the moral capacities of any but the most virtuous individuals, can sustain a system of justice.

It is so important for non-Roman Christianity to build a real community in which the treasures of faith and life can be borrowed and exchanged for many reasons; but in the field of social ethics it is particularly important because the freedom which emerged from the disintegration of the medieval synthesis of biblical and classical modes of thought created so many complementary and contradictory emphases, that only a genuine sharing can bring together the achievements of various parts of the Church and can garner the insights of the various post-medieval centuries.

Let us view the necessity of a new synthesis first in terms of the political and economic organization of the parochial, that is, national community. One of the hazards of the early Reformation, both Lutheran and Calvinistic, was that the new realism, derived from a Pauline and Augustinian estimate of the sinfulness of all men and discarding the semi-Pelagianism which supported the medieval political ethic, naturally but dangerously assigned a purely negative function to the political order. It was an order of constraint designed to 'keep sin in check'. Luther's 'earthly kingdom' was a realm of 'chains, laws, courts and the sword'. In short it was a restrictive order. The only norm of justice was Luther's '*Billigkeit*' or sense of equity. Since the papal authority over the Civil state was naturally disavowed, the moral norms for criticizing positive law and contemporary institutions were obscured.

The excessive emphasis on Paul's admonition in Romans 13 to be 'subject to the higher powers' because they are ordained of God and 'a terror to the evil and not to the good', an admonition which had its own contemporary relevance in warning against eschatological irresponsibility with respect to civil authority, had the historical consequence of obscuring the moral ambiguity of political authority and of the political order in general.

The moral ambiguity of the political and economic order is in fact one of the perennial facts of man's collective existence which required ages of experience before the Christian conscience could be sufficiently at home in this milieu to act responsibly in it. The Early Church, with its eschatological perfectionism and political irresponsibility could be negative toward and critical of, the functions of government; and its radical stewardship doctrine or 'distributive communism,' derived from the time when members 'were of one heart and soul' and laid 'all their possessions at the apostles' feet', made the Early Church critical of property. Government and property were in fact the two morally ambiguous instruments for establishing a tolerable peace and order in a community of self-seeking men. The moral ambiguity of these instruments was due to the fact that they both established peace and created injustice. The conservative impulses of Christianity, first expressed in St Paul, tended to be unduly appreciative of them as instruments of order, while the more radical versions of the faith were unduly critical of them because they imagined a more perfect humanity which would obviate their necessity.

The Catholic tradition had its own way of dealing with this paradox, which need not concern us, except provisionally. It expressed the radical criticism of the institution of property by the voluntary poverty of the monastics; and the critical attitude toward government by reverence for the Church as a 'perfect society' from the standpoint of which it was possible to be critical of all secular government. Thus Gregory the Great could say, 'The kings have their dominion by perfidy and plunder' and Augustine, whose *De Civitate Dei* laid the foundation for Christian political realism, truly described the *civitas terrena* as an uneasy armistice between competitive political forces and the dominance of one force, which created order, as fleeting benefit. The governors of the world will not have their authority long 'for they used it not well while they had it.' Augustine was more critical of government than Luther. For him it was not an ordinance of God, but the momentary results of the victory of one political faction over another. This faction would inevitably offend the divine majesty by ultimate pretensions unlawful for sinful men. Some of the critical equalitarianism, borrowed from Chrysostom, and ultimately derived from Stoicism, is expressed in Augustine's sentiment 'Hence the holy men of old were shepherds of cattle rather than kings of men.'

The Augustinian political realism was gradually eroded in the medieval period as the Church, after Gregory VII, established dominion over the whole of western Christendom as the senior partner of a complicated arrangement in which the junior partner was the western empire which the Pope constructed by crowning Charlemagne Emperor. Augustine's qualms about the identification of the Church with the *Civitas Dei*, were forgotten in Gregory VII's simple identification of the all-powerful Church with the city of God; and even the political realism, derived from Augustine's description of the uneasy balances of power in the political realm, was obscured in the complacent assumption that the dominance of the institution of grace over the political institution would cure the latter of its moral ambiguity.

The Protestant Reformation was primarily a religious protest against the conceptions of grace in the medieval Church. But in terms of our immediate interests in social ethics it was a protest against the political pretensions of an overarching sovereignty which had distilled political power from the prestige of sanctity and had used its alleged possession of the 'keys of heaven' to unlock the doors of political dominion. The protest was well taken. But it is not usually observed that the Reformation, opening a new chapter in Christianity's approach to the moral ambiguities of the political order, frequently aggravated, rather than clarified the fact that there were in fact two almost distinct protestant movements, the classical Reformation of Luther and Calvin, and the radical sectarian protestantism of the Anabaptists of the sixteenth century and the Cromwellian sects of the seventeenth century in England.

The classical Reformation of Luther and Calvin was informed by a political conservatism, strongly influenced by Luther's emphasis on the Pauline doctrine of Romans 13. It gave extravagant reverence to political authority as ordained by God. It tended to assign political authority a purely negative function of restraining self-seeking men and maintaining order. There were differences of course between Luther's and Calvin's theories of sin and grace and providence and even in their view of the state. Calvin was more concerned to prevent tyranny by providing for a tension of power in the central power of government; while he also assigned the 'lower magistrates' both the right and the duty to resist the tyrant. But both Reformers were inclined to ascribe injustice in the political order to a divine punishment for the sins of the victims of tyranny and to look for deliverance to providence.

The radical sects, on the other hand, approached the moral ambiguities of both the political and economic order from an opposite direction. They were inclined to emphasize the evils consequent on both the institutions of property and government. The Anabaptists were quasi-communist and utopian. The Cromwellian sects exhibited every type of social perfectionism, the communism of Gerard Winstanley and the libertarianism of Lilburne and the Levellers and Independents.

Actually all that is cherished in the standard of an 'open society' in western civilization had some roots in the curious blend of left-wing Calvinism and sectarian perfectionism of the seventeenth century. In addition it was necessary to garner those aspects of truth in the political policy of the English Reformation, particularly of the Elizabethan Settlement, so clearly elaborated in Hooker's *Laws of Ecclesiastical Polity* in which the conservative monarchism of Edmund Burke and the liberal theories of John Locke were both present in embryo.

Clearly an ecumenical movement was necessary to garner the diverse and often contradictory fruits of the Reformation ages and create a consistent Protestant attitude toward political reality. It was also necessary to keep the doctrine relevant to current experience as it was influenced by the world-shaking events which began with the First World War. Significantly the first conference on Life and Work which with the other movement on Faith and Order constituted the ecumenical movement, which in turn resulted in the organization of the World Council of Churches in the conference at Amsterdam, was the conference at Stockholm after the First World War. The conference did not fully mirror the crisis in our culture, caused by the First World War. That crisis might be defined as caused by the shaking of the dogmas of the eighteenth and nineteenth centuries, affirming the perfectibility of man and the idea of progress. These dogmas were as potent in religious communities as in secular ones. They had obscured much of the realism which Christianity had contributed to the analysis of the task of preserving a tolerable harmony and justice in a world of sin. Perhaps the triumph of the 'democracies' in the bitter conflict gave the Wilsonian idealism, with its hope of 'making the world safe for democracy', a special prestige. At any rate the Conference breathed the spirit of liberal moralism. There was no evidence of the influence of the more conservative Reformation churches on social theory, perhaps because the defeat of Germany, the national centre of Reformation thought, subdued this witness. Nor is there any evidence of the influence of the redoubtable neo-Reformation theologian, Karl Barth, who after Stockholm had increasing influence on ecumenical thought. In 1925, the year of Stockholm, his rebellion against liberal Protestantism, already expressed in his *Römerbrief*, was yet to be felt.

The economic theory of Stockholm, as expressed in the message, was simply expressed in the words 'We have declared that the soul is of supreme value and must not be subordinated to the rights of property or the mechanisms of industry and that it may claim as its first right, the right of salvation. Therefore we contend for the free and full development of the human personality. . . . Co-operation between capital and labour should take the place of conflict so that employers and employed alike may regard their part in industry as the fulfilment of their vocation.' This Christian individualism and moral idealism hardly came to grips with the problems of a growing industrial civilization. Stockholm could not of course foresee that the Marxist rebellion, initiated in Europe, should have found real lodgement in the defeated Russia after the first World War and that the class conflict in both domestic and international politics was to trouble the world in the next decades, and perhaps centuries.

In the vexing problems of a new international order, which the peace-makers at Versailles tried to solve by accepting Woodrow Wilson's League of Nations, the Conference contented itself with the statement 'We have also set forth the guiding principles of Christian internationalism, equally opposed to national bigotry and weak cosmopolitanism. We have affirmed the universal character of the church and its duty to preach and practise the love of the brethren. . . . We have . . . examined the constitution of an international order, which would provide peaceable methods of removing the causes of war. . . . We summon the churches to share our

horror of war and of its futility as a means of settling international disputes.'

It is of course easy by the wisdom of hindsight, which
incorporates the tragic experiences of a century which had not
one, but two, world wars and is now in the throes of a cold
war and a nuclear dilemma, to be critical of this vague
moralism. But it may not be inappropriate to make the
judgment that Stockholm did not exhaust the full dimensions
of biblical faith in dealing with the social problems of a tragic
age. The encounter between the churches had just begun.

In between the Stockholm and the Oxford conference many
smaller meetings did much spadework in working out a social
ethic. Thus in a conference of Christian social workers, held in
London in 1930, the statement of principles of Christian ethical
concern becomes much more specific. 'In our opinion,'
declares the statement, 'the Christian virtues of love, service
and brotherhood could be effectively implemented upon the
basis of a theory of justice as treated in natural law. We feel
that, although capital is necessary in our complex system of
production, it fails to be held in constant reference to Christian
principles in regard to production, distribution and consump-
tion.'

This statement is not only more specific than that of Stockholm but it profits by the Anglican witness in the ecumenical
encounter, revealed in the reference to 'natural law'. Protestantism, as a whole, has a too lively awareness of historical
contingencies and the unique occasion to accept natural law
theories uncritically; and the Reformation belief that reason is
not exempt from the fall, which is to say that reason may be
the servant of the passion and interests of the self, creates an
awareness of the ideological distortions which creep into even
the most disinterested definitions of moral norms. Nevertheless the emphasis on natural law is creative in Protestant circles
both because it typifies the quest for the most authoritative
general norm; and because natural law conceptions invariably

emphasize justice, rather than order, as the basic norm of political and economic life.

The Oxford conference on Church, Community and State was convened in 1937, in an atmosphere of apprehension created by the rise of the Nazi movement in Germany. But it was not this worsening international situation, which was the primary cause of the greater degree of specificity and urbane Christian wisdom, which distinguished Oxford from Stockholm. Two decades of encounter between the churches and of course the encounter between the churches and the rapidly developing industrial and international crisis, helped the Oxford conference to make history in its comprehensive analyses of the complex problems of the political and economic order.

The Oxford report on 'Church and State' reveals a truly ecumenical and balanced view of political authority in which the negative and positive approaches to the state, characteristic of the two types of Protestantism both come into their own. 'We recognize existing historical states as given historical realities', the report declares, 'each of which is the highest political authority, but which stands itself under the authority and judgment of God. . . . At the same time we recognize that the state, as a specific form and the dominating expression of man's life in a world of sin, often becomes, by its very power and its monopoly of the means of coercion, an instrument of evil. Since we believe in the holy God as a source of justice, we do not consider the state as a source of law but as its guarantor. It is not the lord, but the servant, of justice.'

There were, of course, some unresolved conflicting positions at Oxford, particularly in regard to the authority of the state to wage war. The conference recognized three historic positions on this question: (1) the position of the orthodox Reformation, which gave the state undisputed authority in the use of the sword; (2) the majority position, that the state could wage war in self-defence and in the interests of justice. This position, championed, among others, by Archbishop Temple, perhaps the most influential Christian leader of the conference, was to play an important role in the subsequent 'interventionist' debates which preceded the Second World War; (3) the pacifist attitude toward war, which represented the viewpoint, not only of the historic 'peace churches' but a considerable section of the other churches, was recognized as a legitimate Christian witness. Dr Temple's immense authority did not succeed in persuading the conference to define pacifism as a 'Christian heresy'. Since Oxford the second position has become regnant. The first position was refuted not only by the ecumenical consensus but by the encounter of the Church with Nazism. The pacifist witness has remained, as is proper, a recognized minority witness in the Church.

In dealing with the relation of the love commandment to political and economic structures, Oxford was wise and circumspect. It warned against two errors: 'The one is to regard the realities of justice, incorporated in given systems of order, as so inferior to the law of love, that the latter cannot be a principle of discriminate judgment between them but only a principle of indiscriminate judgment upon them all. . . . The other error is to equate a particular system with the kingdom of God.'

The report wisely suggests that this error leads conservatives to give religious sanction to the *status quo*, and the critics of the *status quo* to give religious sanction to a new system, which, when its defects are revealed, leads to disillusion. The report indicts the prevailing capitalistic system of the Western world for aggravating acquisitiveness and for not correcting flagrant inequalities. It thus points to what has since been achieved in Western democracies in the form of the minimal securities of the welfare state, and the combination of social planning and free initiative of a mixed economy.

The report makes a necessary distinction between the duty to create more perfect structures of justice on the one hand and

The Sufficiency of God

the responsibility of love which transcends any given structure and comprehends the dignity of the person in the most perfect and imperfect of social and economic structures. Finally the report calls for self-criticism of both the groups which are tempted to complacency by their ideological commitment to an established order and the rebellious group who invest an alternative with an ultimate sanction which it cannot deserve.

The conference encouraged Christians to be responsible in a wide variety of social reform efforts but warned that no programme could claim the right to be called 'Christian'. Long before Russian Communism revealed the evils of an omnicompetent state, Oxford warned against simple alternatives of socialization of property to the present system. It declared: 'Recent Russian history warns us of the danger of irresponsible political power supplanting irresponsible economic power, if the democratic control of power is destroyed.'

In short the Oxford conference laid the foundation for what has developed into an impressive system of Christian pragmatism. It is Christian in the sense that the law of love on the one hand and the Christian awareness of the law of self-love as an ubiquitous and persistent force describes the upper and the lower limits of a social order in a sinful world. Love describes the upper limits in two ways. It is a constant principle of discriminate, rather than indiscriminate, judgment upon various structures of justice; and it makes demands upon the individual which transcend every system of justice. The persistence of self-love in any system warns against all utopian illusions, particularly those which derive social evil from a specific source or institution, whether in the economic or political order. The approach is pragmatic in the sense that it becomes increasingly aware of the contingent circumstances of history which determine how much or how little it is necessary to emphasize the various regulative principles of justice, equality and liberty, security of the community or the freedom of the individual, the order of the integral community

124

and, as is now increasingly the case, the peace of the world community.

The first Assembly of the newly organized 'World Council of Churches' embodying both the 'Life and Work' and 'Faith and Order' movements, met in the summer of 1948 at Amsterdam, Holland. The tragic Second World War had ended but a few years and the Communist movement had grown to worldwide proportions. The pressures of current experience and the additional encounter between churches of various viewpoints served to accentuate the note of sober realism in the social doctrines of the ecumenical movement of the non-Roman churches.

The emphasis on 'Middle Axioms', initiated by Archbishop Temple, embodied the truth in the natural law theories, namely the perennial principles of social policy stemming from perennially operative forces in the human community and from the intuitions of justice or the rational calculations and discriminations which seek to make justice into an instrument of the love commandment.

The political dogmas of both right and left, of both 'free enterprise' and 'socialization' are increasingly dissolved by history and common experience. The report on political and economic organization declared 'The Church cannot resolve the debate between those who feel that the primary solution (of the social problem) is the socialization of the means of production and those who fear that such a course will merely lead to new and inordinate combinations of political and economic power' but it is prepared to say 'to the advocates of the socialization of property that the institution is not the root of the corruption of human nature. We must equally say to the defenders of existing property relations that ownership is not an unconditioned right. It must be preserved, curtailed and distributed according to the requirements of justice.'

The report observes that 'the revolt of the multitudes against injustice gives communism much of its strength. . . . Christians who are the beneficiaries of capitalism should try to see the world from the perspective of those who are excluded from its benefits and who see in Communism a means of deliverance from poverty and insecurity.' The Amsterdam report nevertheless goes on: 'The churches should reject the ideologies of both Communism and *laissez-faire* capitalism and should draw men from the false assumption that these extremes are the only alternatives. Each has made promises that it could not fulfil.'

This well-balanced statement, which current history has validated, seemed to many in the west as merely an effort to preserve a balance in the first signs of the 'cold war'. On the other hand there were critics of capitalism who challenged the term '*laissez-faire* capitalism' (incidentally suggested by the distinguished American layman Charles P. Taft) as a way of breaking the impact of the judgment upon western institutions. It was in fact a recognition of the obvious fact that western democracies had slowly corrected the injustices of early industrialism by bringing the freedom in the economic order under progressive moral and political control. The subsequent consistent development of the welfare state and of a mixed economy proved the correctness of a definition of western institutions, which condemned the original dogma but not the present mixed realities. The first Assembly of the World Council expressed in every domain of life and analysis a note of sober realism, a circumspect distinction between the soteriological and ethical dimensions of human existence, of the realms of grace and of law; and a freedom from the political dogmas of the past, which potentially put the ecumenical movement in a reconciling position in the political dogmatic debates which would erupt in the next decades.

The second assembly of the World Council, held in 1954 in Evanston, Illinois, built its social doctrine on the foundations laid in Oxford and Amsterdam. The rapidly developing world situation naturally prompted attention to new areas of concern.

In international problems Evanston particularly commended the United Nations for its declaration of human rights and for its technical assistance programme. It failed, at one point, to anticipate the actual course of international events. It rightly warned against the efforts of the great powers to dominate the organization, despite the constant reiteration of the principle of the 'equal sovereignty' of all states great and small. But it did not prepare the conscience of the churches for the dread realities of the present in which two great powers competitively share responsibility, both for the development of technically backward nations and for the prevention of a dread nuclear holocaust. In one respect the United Nations has however fulfilled the hopes of the Evanston assembly. It has become a forum in which the small nations can fashion world opinion which may ultimately place a check upon the great powers and can furnish the tissue of world community.

The two problems, one age-old and the other new, which engaged Evanston with a new sense of urgency were racial tensions and the desire of the technically undeveloped nations for both political independence and technical competence. Its plea for racial and ethnic brotherhood was uncompromising but, fortunately, not uniquely Protestant. The recent Papal Encyclical *Mater et Magistra* gives witness to the concern of the Catholic church for the universality of the responsibility of brotherhood, inside and outside the Church. And the secular community has frequently contributed to the cause of racial understanding in ways which might shame complacent churches. In this realm it is not necessary for the churches, Roman and non-Roman, to develop a unique social ethic, but merely to make an honest application of the universalistic elements in the Christian ethic.

In the realm of assistance to what became known as 'areas of rapid social change', the World Council since Evanston has broken new ground by establishing a special commission to study and explicate the responsibilities of the churches in those areas of the world in which political independence and the impingement of technical and industrial forms of community upon old, organic forms of community create many new problems while solving the age-old problem and burden of penury. The most recent study by the secretary of the Commission, Dr Paul Abrecht, entitled *The Churches and Rapid Social Change* is an excellent example of the increasing detail with which the ecumenical movement explicates its essential position. The splendid work of this Commission is the last fruit of the growing tendency toward empirical and pragmatic approaches to specific moral and social problems, which is held within the general framework of the love-commandment, the law which fulfils and dissolves all specific laws, fashioned for particular occasions, but soon dated and outmoded by new occasions.

The Protestant and Greek churches cannot claim to have any monopoly of wisdom available to a harassed humanity, living amidst the revolutions of race and nations, and standing under the impending judgment of a nuclear catastrophe, which, in prospect at least, will be of eschatological proportions. They may however modestly claim that their experience of brotherly encounter with each other has enriched the common heritage, overcome the fractional character of various traditions and adjusted and applied the whole to the rapidly changing world situation.

THE CONFESSING CHURCH
AND THE ECUMENICAL
MOVEMENT

Martin Fischer

The Church and the Ecumenical Movement in Germany

WHEN we consider the life of Protestant Christians in Germany we must first remember that the Reformers did not intend to found a new church. For the sake of the one, holy, apostolic Church they were drawn into a struggle with Rome which ended with their exclusion from the Roman church. It was in the name of this one holy apostolic Church that they maintained their own ecclesiastical existence, and concerned themselves with the return of the heretical Roman church to the Gospel. They gloried in the free word of the Holy Scripture which stood over against the Church and made it into a creature of the Word. In all their rejoicing over their own understanding, and the faithfulness of their teaching and life, their decisive aim was to glorify Jesus Christ. They understood their own way only as a means of loyalty toward him who remains alone the Lord of truth.

It was in him that this Church, like every other, was filled with promise. Wherever it tried to secure itself in other ways these efforts became the basis of further tensions and divisions. Where it gloried in the law it found the law, and in human laws the destruction of unity. It maintained unity only in trying to be loyal to the Lord of the one, holy, apostolic Church. Legalism could have made the history of the Church into a history of withdrawals from the Church. Confessional legalism can weld together unity based on certain symbols, but is guilty in so doing of further tensions and splits. Also, culturally homogeneous churches, held together by one political tradition and one political will, can lose in this effort their proper object, faith and life, as many churches in Germany did in the course of the eighteenth century. No confessional position guarantees life. One cannot save manna; it spoils overnight. God wills to be necessary to us every day himself. Where God works, he works in unity, free of our preconditions but in the midst of our situation.

The Awakening which began at the end of the eighteenth century ignored as a rule the variety and limits of existing churches. New impulses went through all churches and groups; and the fruit of these impulses and stimuli was, among other things, the effort of Christians who were ready for union, to do justice in unity to the unified essence and work of their Lord. Even efforts at union to be sure could take on a legalistic tone which only increases divisiveness.[1] They could, however, also be a daring attempt in respect for the divinity of God and the greater unity given in Christ to express the unity which in fact has been given by the working of the Holy Spirit. Living unity which seemed according to doctrinal tradition to be impossible, often became real in the faith of confessing Christians.

The experience of the Christian community has in this sense always been a training ground for ecumenical obligations. It has become so on a world-wide scale since the Awakening impressed its missionary responsibility upon the whole Church. Through this channel have come encounters with other

---

[1] On the problem of union cf. J. W. Winterhager, *Kirchenunionen des 20. Jahrhunderts*, Zürich and Frankfurt/M. 1961; Hans Emil Weber, *Von Recht und Sendung evangelischer Union*, Essen 1935; H. H. Harms, *Bekenntnis und Kircheneinheit bei den jungen Kirchen*, Berlin 1952.

churches, with movements, and with new experiments in Christian obedience. When pietism is called a living movement of the Church this refers to the impulse the Church received therefrom to recognize and accept ecumenical obligations.[1] It is a fact that in Germany many of the decisive impulses and awakenings have cut directly across confessions and churches in their effectiveness. They have not only jumped the borders of churches, they have levelled them, or at least relativized them.

The reaction of serious preaching and teaching in the Church was to reassert these borders, making them seem firmer than was spiritually justified by the faith which had brought them first into being. The German situation in theology and church practice was often made tedious and burdensome by the effort to push the Awakening into the courtyard of the Church, to secure the Church's doctrinal substance, without inquiring in true repentance what the pietist movement's Gospel might have to say to the Church. The nineteenth century was full of spiritual and theological impulses. It was a rich and confusing century in which movements found the way to the Church hard, and the Church found it hard to express itself in movement; in which two ways of thought—one which started from the Church as institution, office and theology, and another which started from human beings, with their spiritual impulses—men used up their strength in continuous, tiring wrestling with one another. Growing nihilism and nationalism were the answer of the world to this powerless use, or idolatrous misuse, of the name of God.[2] A peculiar lethargy brooded over the preaching of the Church in Germany.[3] The spirit of the times was no longer the spirit of Christendom, and the spirit in the Church

[1] Cf. M. Fischer—*Die bleibende Bedeutung des Pietismus*, Witten 1960, pp. 77ff.
[2] W. Lütgert, in *Die Religion des deutschen Idealismus und ihr Ende*, Gütersloh 1923 has given an impressive description of this development.
[3] Alfred Niebergall, 'Die Geschichte der christlichen Predigt', *Leiturgia* Band II, Kassel 1957, esp. pp. 336ff.

which Schleiermacher and his followers had attempted to cultivate so carefully and with so much human concern, dissolved in an ocean of doctrines. In this ocean of doctrines even the one message of the one Lord to his one Church threatened to be drowned.[1]

The Way of the Confessing Church

To combat this breakdown God called his witnesses. After the first World War, but before the church struggle with Nazism started, Germany was equipped by a theological renewal for the trials ahead. In contrast to the resigned spirit of many preachers before this war, we find after the war preachers who have a new theologically-founded certainty. The Confessing Church could later become a preaching movement, just as the Reformers had once so lived, because of this renewal.[2] In theology and in preaching the new impulses of the twentieth century, as of the nineteenth, went straight through churches and confessions. Where the Gospel became effective it stopped at no borders. Just as sins and ideologies run through all churches and confessions, so also worked the healing Word of God without regard for traditions, whether well-founded or questionable. Germany was a field of ecumenical responsibility, even within its own borders, split and torn and at the same time gifted by God with a message through which the believers received a unity which reached beyond all borders. It became ever more clear that the Lutheran preacher does not say what truth is for the Lutherans, nor does the Reformed preacher for the Reformed, and the Pietist for the Pietists, but that there can only be preaching which is loyal to the one Lord who intends it for all, who lays

[1] Cf. Karl Kupisch, *Zwischen Idealismus und Massendemokratie*, Berlin 1955.

[2] See M. Fischer, 'Die Bekennende Kirche als Predigtbewegung' in Festschrift for H. Vogel (*Vom Herrengeheimnis der Wahrheit*), Berlin 1962, pp. 59-87.

claim on all, and who regards traditions and borders only as temporary. This was a gift to the Church, but it was also a danger to the practice of many churches. There were understandably a number of efforts to flee from this danger.[1]

Before questions of this kind could be worked out in Germany, however, the country was plunged into a struggle which tested the whole of Christendom regardless of the various forms in which it expressed its faith. As God had prepared us with the teaching of the Gospel by an offer to all churches, as a false gospel brought a Messianic intoxication over the whole land which became a temptation for all churches and groups, so our salvation lay not in faith in the Church but only in faith in God himself, and his free Gospel.[2] Where this God was worshipped divine services became the scene of battle. Altars were overturned, fear was overcome, and the call to faith and obedience became equally audible in the most varied places. God's word became effective anew as a unifier, so that Christians of the most various backgrounds recognized each other as Christians, and found a common faith and confession which they shared to the limit of martyrdom and death. We could not withdraw from the battle—and therefore from the offer of the Gospel—by silence, by retreat into liturgy, or by ambiguous confessional statements and agreements, such as shielded parts of the Church from the interference of anti-Christian state power for a time.[3] Under such circumstances one fell out of the community of confessors even when one seemingly remained loyal to the confession.

[1] For documentation of the Church Struggle cf. Karl Barth, *Theological Existence Today*, London 1933; H. Asmussen, 'Kirche der Augsburger Konfession' (Heft 16) and 'Barmen!' (Heft 24), *Theologische Existenz Heute*, Munich 1934-1935. See also, controversy with Hermann Sasse, 'Hans Asmussen und das Luthertum' in *Allgemeine Evangelisch-Lutherische Kirchenzeitung* 25 and 26, Leipzig 1936.

[2] Thus (despite his criticism of the Confessing Church in some particulars) R. Hermann in *Theologische Anliegen zur Kirchenfrage*, Greifswald 1937.

[3] Opposing this tendency see the impressive argument of G. Jacob, *Die Versuchung der Kirche*, Göttingen 1947.

Where we truly confessed we found a unity beyond confessional statements; we sought and found a living confession: for example, in 1934, the theological declaration of Barmen, in which the differences between Lutheran and Reformed congregations and theologians became recognizable and bearable as temporary distinctions within a common faith and confession.[1] The opponent and the Lord of all these theological struggles brought us together. We received a new impulse to ecumenical unity.

There was, however, a danger in this. There arose under the pressure of the state and in the joy of common worship, a strong understanding of the Church influenced by the romantic concept of organism, but with the confession as the constituting principle.[2] As the young Bonhoeffer put it in a daring formulation: 'Christ existing as congregation.'[3] As distrust of the Nazi state grew (often distrust of the state as such) there arose more and more an exaltation of the Church, as if it might commend itself as the indubitable, incarnate Holy Spirit.[4] One can endanger the Church not only by spiritualizing it (Sohm, and E. Brunner), but also by glorifying it.

We had to fight on two fronts for the witness of the visible Church.[5] Whoever neglected the preaching and order of the Church out of scepticism or emotionalism, had to be confronted with the fact that '*extra ecclesiam nulla salus.*' Where this visible Church, however, became a self-pleasing master, not servant of the word, Luther's angry sentence was more

[1] Cf. Ernst Wolf, *Barmen; Kirche zwischen Versuchung und Gnade*, Munich 1957.

[2] This goes back to Schleiermacher. Cf. Ernst Wolf, *Peregrinatio, Studien zur reformatorischen Theologie und zum Kirchenproblem*, München 1954; pp. 146-82 and 279-301.

[3] Dietrich Bonheoffer, *Sanctorum Communio* (Engl. trs. London 1963).

[4] Cf. R. Hermann, 'Zum evangelischen Begriff der Kirche' in *Gesammelte Studien zur Theologie Luthers und der Reformation*, Göttingen 1960, pp. 342-66.

[5] Cf. M. Fischer, 'Theologie und Kirchenleitung', in *Evangelische Theologie* 21/1961, Heft 2, pp. 49-67.

appropriate, '*abscondita est ecclesia, latent sancti.*'[1] Our task was to remain true to God in the visible Church, to love her in her poverty, and to keep her witness open always for better efforts at humanly responsible teaching and order. All these are insights which also have their value in the worldwide ecumenical community.

The Confessing Church and the Ecumenical Movement: with Prefigurations in Youth Organizations

For a long period during these days the fellowship of the Church in Germany with churches beyond her borders was threatened within and nearly terminated without. The hesitant beginnings of participation in the ecumenical movement during the decade of the '20s became suspect after 1933 as weakness of national character, and later as treasonable liaison with the enemy. Ecumenical contacts were, for those who demanded national isolation, signs of 'internationalism', and decision for 'morbid western democracy'. Whoever stood by the ecumenical movement in these years had to maintain his confession against the intoxication of national idolatry. The ever-increasing isolation of Germany under the ideology of National Socialism confronted the Christians in Germany with the choice—worship of the one Lord who works in all the world, or of the Baal of isolation. With the Church's 'No' to the enemies of the Gospel came a 'Yes' to this ecumenical confession. Probably Germany's church has never been so ecumenically oriented as in the years when its contacts with non-German churches were forcibly halted. Secret visits, even during time of war, bore witness to the unbroken though sorely tested will of the Church of Jesus Christ toward unity.

We would not have adequately described the pre-history of ecumenical work in Germany if we did not also mention the

[1] M. Luther in *De Servo Arbitrio* (On the Bondage of the Will); *WA* 18, p. 652. Cf. H. J. Iwand, 'Zur Entstehung von Luthers Kirchenbegriff' in *Festschrift* for Günther Dehn, 1957.

significance of youth and student work. These movements, children of the Awakening, active from the beginning in supra-confessional scope, turned also from their early general Christian impulses to the need of their Church. The present General Secretary of the World Council of Churches, whom this volume honours, has served both the World YMCA, and later the World's Student Christian Federation in leading positions, and also in Germany his first contacts were with German youth. He became their comrade, their companion in their discoveries, their temptations and problems. Through them he gained quick contact with the struggling Confessing Church in Germany, and he lured them beyond the uncommitted general Christian movement into the acceptance of true co-responsibility for the churches.

In fact, the German Student Christian Union, later the Evangelical Student Congregation, became, through its testing in the church struggle, a training ground for movements of renewal, especially the Confessing Church. A student movement which arose out of the Awakening, the German Student Christian Union, entered the Confessing Church practically in full numbers after being prohibited by the Third Reich. After 1945 it no longer sought a separate existence, but without surrendering its character as movement accepted a position within the church.[1] The Evangelical Student Congregation in Germany is a model for undertakings which know, and do not flee from, the tension between the Church and the churches; but attempt in co-responsibility for the life of the churches, to form and ever re-form a community which lives in hope. The Student Congregation became a unique case in church order. It was criticized on the one side by the established churches for its insufficient subjection to their administration and confession: and at the same time by the World's Student Christian Federation for its insufficient freedom of movement.

Finally, however, this undertaking which arose out of the

[1] Cf. M. Fischer in *Wegemarken*, Berlin 1959, pp. 181-229 and 114-31.

difficult struggles of the Confessing Church, not only found silent toleration but set a certain ecumenical example beyond the borders of Germany. Here the institutional church and the missionary movement were not torn apart. They were not even separated into an official church which celebrates the Holy Communion and a missionary forecourt, as if one were not allowed to missionize in the church of the Holy Communion, nor to hold Holy Communion in the forecourt of mission.[1] Rather here the effort was made to hold the borders of the Church open for new action of God in his Word; and at the same time to support the Church with a sacrifice and dedication never before known in our state church past.

Dr W. A. Visser 't Hooft and the Confessing Church in Germany

It is appropriate at this point to remember the man who kept the ecumenical movement close to the struggling Confessing Church by continual contacts during the difficult years of the church struggle. Dr Visser 't Hooft was not only wonderfully suited for this task by brotherly friendship with those who carried responsibility for the Church, and especially with those who had risen out of the student work, he was also equipped by a high degree of historical and theological education. On the one hand he had been so much a part of the theological renewal after the First World War that he remained prepared to accept theological criticism and not to suspect it, or dismiss it as intellectualism. On the other hand he was important to the theological youth of our land because he resisted their self-pleasing over-estimation of correct theological discoveries as long as these discoveries did not prove themselves in responsible practice.

He gave courage to us Germans who so often strain after pedantic completeness, not to neglect church action and confession because we had not yet worked out the full theological

[1] Cf. in contrast with W. Maurer my essay; 'Die bleibende Bedeutung des Pietismus', *op. cit.*, pp. 79ff.

explanation of it. He participated as few other foreigners in the give and take of theologically responsible action in Germany, such as did not take flight into the hardening, or proliferation of theological ideas, or into resignation about church politics. He himself called the forming of the Confessing Church the great ecumenical event of our time, and contributed to maintaining it and making it effective. He knew himself to be in one boat with the struggling brothers of the Confessing Church, and he entered this boat many times in the hours of danger. He was prepared for joyful recognition, but also for sharp criticism, which was most clearly given to his friends. It was usually well-grounded. There is no doubt that his German friends must often deeply have disappointed him, but because he belonged to the real Church with its weaknesses and sins, not to an ideal church, he remained loyal also to those who failed.[1]

Here as in many places in the earth he was able patiently to wait until brothers who had gone questionable ways found the freedom to repent (for example, of prejudices and doctrinaire positions, of fixations on national honour and pride, of depressing self-pity and unworthy self-justification) and allowed themselves again to be drawn into co-operation. This kind of patience nourishes itself with great hope. In no other way is it possible to work with a Christendom so filled with reaction and lethargy. In no other way is it possible to overcome self-righteousness and prejudice. Even when Visser 't Hooft saw what was required more clearly than the brethren in Germany itself, he did not present it as a law (he would thus only have solidified the resistance of the reactionaries), but rather he bore witness to the loyalty of the Lord of the Church and brought

[1] We met by chance in Tübingen as the first news came through of the burning of synagogues in Germany. Visser 't Hooft was angry at the slow, paralysed reaction of his German friends. But a few hours later in Heidelberg, I was witness to the protest of Pastor Hermann Maas and his whole congregation in their service of worship against these events. This too was Germany. Cf. *Durchkreuzter Hass* (Heinrich Grüber zum 70ten Geburtstag) Berlin 1961.

reports of struggling brethren in other parts of the world.

Thus he raised the eyes of the Confessing Church in Germany beyond its own battle-field. He remained also close to her in the testing time of war. He did not remove the Geneva office of the World Council of Churches to America, as he was advised to do on grounds of security. He remained in Europe in order to be near to the struggling churches and the suffering peoples, a decision which proved to be fundamental for the whole ecumenical movement. So it became, not the American alternative to a temporary European community, but a free common movement of churches in quite different situations and problems; of churches in victorious and vanquished lands; of young and old churches; of state churches and free denominations, which were called together to attempt a new way.

Dr Visser 't Hooft remained close to the German brethren with this decision. This meant a double burden upon him. On the one side the Confessing Church in Germany was also caught up in the guilt of its people. On the other side it showed modest evidence of maintaining a faith and confession which remained important for all warring peoples in spite of the passion of the battle, and despite the questionable light in which even the Confessing Church in Germany must appear. In spite of many difficult experiences, and despite the pain which Visser 't Hooft as a Dutch patriot must have borne, he remained bound to the Christians in Germany with a brotherhood which was ready to forgive; and after the war he came to them immediately. He welcomed the Stuttgart Confession of Guilt with a warm heart because it gave him back his brothers. The ecumenical movement, under the influence of Dr Bell, Dr Visser 't Hooft and many others, found itself ready in faith in the forgiveness of God to accept the Stuttgart Confession of Guilt as the occasion of God's forgiveness, and to dare to base its work on the community thus given to the Church anew.

Thus was community maintained in times of its greatest

danger, even in times when contact was not possible, and every man had to do his duty in his own place. The community of faith was built on the free spirit of the free God. This did not exclude wrestling for the obedience of one's brother, even to the point of correcting him with cutting sharpness. Visser 't Hooft seemed to soft spirits like a man of cold passion. His friendship was not an emotional pleasure of the human spirit, but completely a service to the common object. This put him in a position not to give up hope, even when faced with stubborn resistance in the years of unspeakable trial. His was a burning passion, a very sober, effective intoxication, or an intoxicated sobriety.

Relevant Theology and Practice

A profound theological decision was the basis of this. In ecumenical work—and Visser 't Hooft has not unjustly been called the engineer of the ecumenical movement—there can be no unity without truth, and no truth without the will to submit oneself to unity in Christ. The widest differences among churches must not become the occasion of resignation, but rather of faith in unity against all appearances for Christ's sake. Confidence in the Spirit of God does not lead to inaction, but to action. It does not content itself with high-flying theological research and ecclesiastical planning, which come to earth only in some period of the past, but takes hold of present problems, looking toward the Lord who lures his Church out of the houses of the past onto the frontiers of new testing and promise.[1] German scholarship tends to find only that research relevant which is presented in written form. Efforts to draw on the lessons of history to diagnose our present time are often resented in the name of science. Something of the owl of Minerva characterizes the German mind. But there are profound theological reasons why the ecumenical movement cannot allow the look backwards to be its only orientation,

[1] Cf. Hans Hoekendijk, 'On the Way to the World of Tomorrow', *Laity*, No. 11, Geneva, August 1961.

why it rather must call our theological efforts toward the frontier of new theologically responsible practice. It is because Christ not only meets the Church as a divine event in her past but also approaches her out of the future which also belongs to God, that the practical obedience of the Church can often mean a purification of her teaching. The Confessing Church was forced by the painful leading of God to this purification, and learned therein that where a church is subjected to these pains, there it is blessed.

Visser 't Hooft has been described as having the gifts of a statesman.[1] These are not only gifts of nature, but come also from theological understanding. The great capacity to listen carefully, to let buildings stand for the time being, and yet to build new tents, to be under iron control and yet feverishly expectant of what the future will bring, all this is the reflection of a calling which has been that of the Confessing Church and of the engineers of the ecumenical movement. It has been an important lesson for the German church in its co-operation in the World Council of Churches to learn the art of moderation, which is so difficult for Germans: the art of the possible and the art of placing the impossible, or the not yet possible, in the background, without giving up the expectation that that which is not possible now may one day become so.

Church and Movement

Not a few friends of Visser 't Hooft were concerned lest the ecumenical movement lose its character as movement and become churchified, just as many in Germany were concerned lest the movement of the Awakening might fall to ecclesiasticism.[2] What lay behind this anxiety? Mainly the unhappy heritage of a spiritualized concept of the Church, and a positivistic concept of order such as we have been concerned

[1] M. Niemöller, 'Von Evanston nach Neu-Delhi, Ökumene in Rückblick und Ausblick', *Ökumenische Rundschau* 2, April 1961.

[2] Cf. M. Fischer, 'Pietismus und Kirche in der christlichen Studentenbewegung', *Theologie und Pietismus*, Neukirchen 1961, pp. 48-59.

to conquer. We were afraid that in place of men bound together in faith in a daring movement, experts in church administration and ecclesiastical representatives might appear, bringing with them problems which have already been solved in principle. We were afraid that thus those people who desire to push missionary-oriented, relevant Christian life as far as possible from the duly constituted church, would once again take over.[1] We knew too well the academic theologians and simple awakened Christians, who were either too elegant or too pious to fight for the visible Church, and the churchmen who seemed to be satisfied so long as teaching and administration remained untouched, even if there were no congregations. We had seen all of these people fail in the time of testing, and had recognized that they could only stand then and now under the long outmoded protection of a *corpus Christianum*, not in the reality of a nihilistic or atheistic world. We were concerned for believing congregations and for a churchly existence which would not spare itself the test of confessing by making peace with the attackers, or depending on protecting powers.

When there was no possibility of direct co-operation, however, we never lost our confidence in Visser 't Hooft and his colleagues. Old fellowship in the movement helped to ride out the crisis. The participation of the German churches in the ecumenical movement was prepared in the Confessing Church.[2] There we learned that God can call people anew, and even set churches in movement. And so we experienced the fact that awakening and true theology in Germany and in the ecumenical movement lead toward responsible, constructive work in the Church and that affirmation of the Church cannot annul the elements of movement.

[1] This problem was most strongly stated in Emil Brunner, *The Misunderstanding of the Church*, London 1952. Cf. Karl Barth's criticism: *Church Dogmatics* IV/2.
[2] Cf. the well informed report of H. Böhm, 'Bekennende Kirche und Ökumene', *Bekennende Kirche, Martin Niemöller zum 60ten Geburtstag*, Munich 1952, pp. 191-7.

What seemed impossible seems now to have become possible in the World Council of Churches: that young men out of the movement can work alongside representatives of highly organized churches with the will that the Church of Jesus Christ may become one. Though we feared the ecumenical movement would become predominantly a trading place for ecclesiastical interests, and that thereby the open field of the future would be enclosed, we found rather that a miracle happened. These churches and their representatives have been set in movement, and have allowed themselves to be swept along as equally amazed participants in the real challenges and deeds of the Spirit of God today. The ecumenical movement owes this opening of the Church for necessary and possible steps into the future, not to emotional fireworks but to the patient work of persuasion which sober men have carried out, who sought to serve the deeds and tendencies of the Spirit of God in the world of our time. This confidence has not been disappointed. Many churches have become mobile. History has not been set aside in the process. The World Council of Churches has become more than a 'clerical Rotary Club'. It has simply taken up the offer of the Spirit, the possibilities offered to perform obedient, careful and—considering their significance in world history—remarkably unpretentious deeds. It has remained in touch with young and old churches. The next decades will tell what influence this will have on the theology and the order of individual churches. Already Erik Wolf has been able, as fruit of the theology and practice of the Confessing Church in Germany, to develop a proposal for the order of the Church on an ecumenical basis, thereby making a substantial contribution to all the churches in the world, even when they at many points would differ from his proposals.[1] It is the meaningful consequence of the leading

[1] Erik Wolf, *Ordnung der Kirche, Lehr- und Handbuch des Kirchenrechts auf ökumenischer Basis*, Frankfurt/M 1961. Along with his older works—*Rechtsgedanke und Biblische Weisung*, Tübingen 1947, and *Recht des Nächsten,*

which God has given the Church that the missionary movement which grew out of the Awakening flows into ecclesiastical responsibility, and that the Church is prepared to take the missionary movement into itself, as was expressed in the organizational union of the World Council of Churches and the International Missionary Council at New Delhi. The history of the Confessing Church in Germany is part of the background of this event.

Church and Politics

The Confessing Church in Germany could not avoid politics. It was tempted many times to limit the church struggle to purely spiritual decisions, and to misuse the doctrine of the two realms, to render the preaching of the Church sterile, and to concern itself in its confession only with the task of maintaining the Church.[1] Representatives of the Ecumenical Movement outside Germany observed with all the more interest therefore the important efforts of the German Confessing Church to obey the commandments of God in the area of political decision. The theological equipment of the Church for this task was extraordinarily weak. The worship of the national Baal which had permeated her preaching during the First World War, was far from eliminated despite the theological renewal of the 'twenties and the 'thirties. Pietistic circles, on the other hand, often failed in their responsibility for man in his common life, with the excuse that they were engaged in 'purely spiritual' work.[2] The Confessing Church met one defeat after another in this area until finally a whole people was forced to

1958, this basic work is, in the opinion of a Lutheran critic, 'a comprehensive presentation which upholds and impressively reaffirms the tradition of German church law' (S. Grundmann).

[1] Cf. Ernst Wolf, 'Kirchenkampf', *Religion in Geschichte und Gegenwart 3* III, col. 1443-1453, and 'Bekennende Kirche', *ibid.* I, col. 984-988. On the same subject F. W. Marquardt, *Kirche der Menschen*, Berlin 1960.

[2] Cf. R. von Thadden-Trieglaff, *Auf verlorenem Posten?*, Tübingen 1948, pp. 45ff.

recognize the depth of criminal perversity into which its government had led it for lack of adequate resistance. The man who loves cannot avoid politics. The Stuttgart Confession of Guilt was right when it spoke of Germans as being lacking in love.

After the war we faced a new situation which has made the German Church once again an ecumenical, political problem. The new period is characterized by the task which has been given the Church by the division of Germany. This has never been a merely national problem, although even as such it would have concerned the Church, but rather an ideological problem. In this form it is not only a German but an international concern. The border which has been drawn through Germany not only divided two parts of one people, but claimed these two parts for different systems. These systems attempted then not only to develop themselves politically, but to create each a new man, the man of the Christian West, or the man of an atheistic, communistic world-view. The one decisive counter-argument against this division of the world has been the existence of the Church in East and West. The task which has been given to the Church in this is terribly difficult, and the temptation is great to give up the struggle in East and in West, and to obscure the calling of a Church with one faith and duty beneath the practical possibilities of effective work such as are given so abundantly in the West, and in such limited form in the East. Here we have been tempted to claim the Church for the area of the Christian West, and to question the possibility of its existence in the East. We have been tempted furthermore to proclaim Christianity as the means of political integration for the West, after the bitter experience of the Third Reich. On the other side, in the eastern part of Germany Christendom could count on understanding and confidence for a while, because of the respect which the Confessing Church had won during Hitler's time. This understanding and confidence had two enemies: one, the growing atheistic influence in the Eastern political world, which led to treating political loyalty as insufficient so long as it was not combined with the complete acceptance of an atheistically determined ideology; and two, the claim of the West over the Church which could only amount to leaving Christians in Eastern realms to their liquidation. For when Christians in the West campaigned only for their own realm and became known at the same time as the sworn enemies of Communism, they strengthened the anti-Church reaction in the politics of the East for the destruction of Christians.[1]

The border drawn through Germany, therefore, not only cut through the body of a people formed by a long history whose most recent episode was the guilt of National Socialism, it also divided large parts of the world into a Communist and an anti-Communist area. It became, therefore, a challenge to the Church to think ecumenically in a way which will be destroyed neither by Communism nor by anti-Communism.

It was not simply national self-importance, therefore, which moved us to interest the churches in the ecumenical movement in the German situation, but concern for a world problem.

The history of the Synods of the Evangelical Church in Germany, and of some regional synods in the provinces, is an impressive example of the new task of the Confessing Church, and the growing difficulty of its work to realize the fruits of its confession.[2] The absorption of Germany into East and West blocs undertaken at first against the will of the people, and the efforts, which also came at first from outside, to press weapons into the hands of the people again, seemed to promise to both parts of Germany a kind of growing sovereignty (within their respective blocs, to be sure) as the one possibility of

[1] Cf. M. Fischer, *Wegemarken*, pp. 264-347.
[2] For an overall picture see G. Heidtmann (ed.) *Kirche in Kampf der Zeit*, Berlin 1954. This is a collection of the messages, statements and words of counsel of the Evangelical Church in Germany with special reference to the East, 1946-54. Cf. also Kurt Scharf (ed.), *Festschrift für Heinrich Vogel*, Berlin 1962.

existence. This loss of unity was deepened by a large number of decisions. The renunciation of national responsibility became the basis of a new nationalism under Western or Eastern aegis. Slogans we thought we had outgrown found a new echo. Added to them were the slogans of friends in East and West, and suggestions that it would be the German contribution to a necessary peace for her to accept the border between the Federal Republic and the DDR as a boundary of peace. It was in this politically hopeless and ideologically neurotic situation that the Church had to maintain its message. We had to impress upon ourselves the ecumenical duty to see that no national ideological difference break the unity of the baptized. Baptized Christians are nearer to one another by their baptism than the members of families, nations, classes and ideologies. If this is true, and every confession of the Church so names it, it has consequences for ecumenical action.

The ecumenical movement is able to bring people within hearing distance of one another, who in God are one humanity, and in Christ one in faith. Either the Lord's Prayer of the baptized in every land leads to the question of a greater possible oneness, or it is a misuse of the name of God. Our 'Yes' to ecumenical responsibility in Germany is the fruit of painful experience. It does not wish to appear as political illusion, but it seeks to demonstrate the reality of God's offer to all men amid and above the misery and guilt of confused peoples.

ECUMENICAL SOCIAL
THINKING IN A CHANGING
WORLD

Paul Abrecht

IT has been said that 'the World Council of Churches manifests to a remarkable extent the sense of responsibility of the
churches for the fateful social issues of our time.' A great
share of the credit for this must go to W. A. Visser 't Hooft,
whom this volume honours. Not only the acceptance by the
ecumenical movement of responsibility for social, economic
and political problems, but also the form in which the responsibility has been expressed bear the marks of his deep personal
interest in this area of ecumenical endeavour, his inspiration
and insight. The searching, pioneering spirit which has
characterized ecumenical social thought is very largely a
result of his concern to see the churches grapple with the real
problems of the world; the biblically inspired realism about
man and society and the restless questioning of the entangling
alliances between Church and world are the special marks of
his contribution.

The question we must ask in this essay (and it is the kind of
question which Visser 't Hooft himself would most likely ask)
is, 'Is the ecumenical understanding of Christian responsibility
in society adequate for the newly emerging world?'

One characteristic of ecumenical social thought has been its capacity to cope with new situations and problems. Over the years there have been fundamental changes in the direction of ecumenical statements on social questions. Alterations in the theological and social climate have obliged the churches to rethink their position at many points. In the early years, during the Life and Work era of 1925-37 much time had to be spent in justifying the right of the Church to speak to the problems of the social order. The fundamental aim of the 1937 Oxford Conference on Church, Community and State was to set forth the theological and biblical basis of ecumenical social ethics. The principal concern during this period was to struggle against two tendencies: on the one hand, the complacency, the isolationism and the individualistic pietism which prevented many Christians from fulfilling their task in society, and on the other, the tendency to interpret the social concern of the Church in such an idealistic way that the true function of the Church in society was distorted. The task of setting forth the concerns of the Church for society in that intellectual and theological climate was not an easy one. In their own volume for the Oxford Conference, J. H. Oldham and W. A. Visser 't Hooft concluded that on this and other questions an ecumenical consensus would be difficult to achieve. They wrote: 'The preparatory work for the Oxford Conference has brought forth such a variety of divergent and conflicting views on all the subjects that have been studied that it is difficult to find one's way through the maze. . . . A full and satisfying treatment of the questions (which divide Christians) . . . would require the labour of many years. . . .' (*The Church and Its Function in Society*, p. 121.)

It is therefore all the more surprising to see how quickly a sufficient number of these difficulties were overcome to enable the ecumenical movement to discover the grounds for a creative and imaginative Christian witness. It is just because of such achievements in the past and because of the dynamic character of ecumenical social thinking that we today must be prepared to respond to the question which is the subject of this essay.

That question is asked by some who fear that institutionalism or ecclesiastical arterio-sclerosis is weakening the vigour and the flexibility of the ecumenical body. It is even suggested in some circles, particularly amongst youth, that 'an ecumenical-establishment mentality', is already overtaking the ecumenical movement and so dissipating the prophetic spirit of ecumenical social thinking that it will be incapable of responding effectively to the new situation we face (or indeed even of recognizing that we confront a new situation).

The specific questions which have been most often raised in this connection and which we must consider are the following:

1. Does ecumenical social thinking have the necessary theological and biblical foundations to enable it to interpret the human condition and the Christian responsibility in relation to the kind of world social problems which confront us?

2. Can the ecumenical movement evolve the new terms of interpretation necessary for a universal witness on the problems of the emerging world society, a witness free from the taint of Western cultural, economic and political bias?

3. Is the thinking of the churches still so much influenced by old social and ideological conflicts that they cannot see the possibilities for the 'new and creative solutions to the problems of justice, order and freedom' which the changing situation opens up to them?

4. Will ecumenical social thinking be able to remain lay-centred, or will it succumb to various factors inevitably tending toward clericalism, e.g. the demand for greater theological competence requiring more professional theologians, or the clerical bias of ecclesiastical organizations?

It is impossible to take up all these questions here. And, in the last analysis, time alone will tell whether ecumenical study and discussion of social questions will prepare the ecumenical movement for the challenge of the future. But at this stage it may be useful to sift through some of the arguments and attitudes underlying these questions and to suggest some of the points which deserve serious attention as the future course of ecumenical social thinking is being determined.

I. *The Challenge to New Theological Reflection in Ecumenical Social Ethics*

Discussion of the theological basis of ecumenical social thought has been, is now, and undoubtedly will remain in the future a necessary and yet paradoxical aspect of ecumenical study. As Visser 't Hooft once pointed out: 'Our understanding of the function of the Church in society and of its relation to the Community and the State depends in the last resort on our doctrine, or our undefined and unconscious assumptions, regarding the relation of the Church to the world.' It is also true however that the formulation of Christian social thought and action cannot, and need not, await complete doctrinal or theological agreement. There are also problems of interpretation which seem to defy solution. We must sympathize with the young British layman, who reported as follows on his impressions of the theological debates in the drafting committee of the Section on Social Affairs at the Evanston Assembly (where the theological discussions were focussed on the Assembly theme, the Christian Hope):

> 'It is possible to achieve some sort of agreement about many aspects of the Christian Hope and it is equally possible to achieve a general measure of agreement among Christians as to how they are to look at the concrete issues. But it is quite impossible to achieve agreement as to how the conclusions follow from the theologians' premises. This may disturb the theologians, but it remains a fact that Christians will agree about the functions of the state and the dangers of state action, about the pressing economic problems of our day, and about their attitude toward communism, while they disagree about the principles used to reach these conclusions. Some may want to use a form of

natural law thinking, even if they do not like to call it so. Others derive their conclusions more directly from the insights of biblical theology and prefer to buttress their attitudes with biblical texts. Some derive their approach from middle axioms based on the doctrines of creation and the incarnation; others have found the Second Coming a justification for inspired social action. The section did not openly broach these thorny topics; had they done so it is unlikely that any report would have been written in view of the limited time available.'[1]

Such remarks will not deter the theologians from their appointed role as guardians of doctrinal purity. Indeed they only confirm many of their worst fears! It makes them all the more concerned to challenge the doctrinal basis of all such concerns.

Today the theological critique of ecumenical social ethics comes from at least three distinct groups:

1. Those theologians, especially the followers of Professor Bultmann, who stress uniquely the ultimate significance of the action of God in Jesus Christ and refuse all attempts at interpreting history, practically reducing the historical dimension to the inner history of the self. Thus they are inclined to attack the grounds of all social ethics when viewed in terms of Christian responsibilities for actual social problems. (There is, however, a small group of left-wing Bultmannites, if that description is appropriate for men like Professor Hans Werner Bartsch, who affirm that 'the preaching of the eschatological message must apply to the social realm and is not at all to be understood only as a private act of individual faith'.)

2. Another group, representing a variety of theological traditions, are united by a desire to develop a more biblically based social ethics, and they challenge the ecumenical movement and the World Council in particular on the grounds that its social ideas reflect a hidden if not an explicit natural law basis. Thus far this group has not reached agreement among themselves about the nature of a more biblical social ethics.

[1] Denys Munby.

3. A third group includes primarily younger theologians of Africa, Asia and Latin America who challenge much of contemporary Christian social thinking on the grounds that it is incapable of dealing with the questions posed by the political, social and cultural situation in the countries outside the West.

Undoubtedly all these groups raise serious questions which reflect vital spiritual problems relating Christianity to the modern social situation, and their voices must be heard in the ecumenical discussion. The Christian existentialists mirror much popular dissatisfaction with the organized, controlled character of our societies. The desire to find meaning in the personal self and its future seems to find a response in a new emphasis on the world to come as revealed in 'Jesus Christ, the eschatological event'. Professor Bultmann raises for the Church in a radical way the whole question of the Christian interpretation of history when he writes: 'Man who complains, "I cannot see meaning in history and therefore my life, interwoven in history, is meaningless" is to be admonished: Do not look around yourself into universal history, you must look into your own personal history.'

The critics of any natural law thinking in their turn raise fundamental questions about the meaning of the World Council's key idea of the Responsible Society and ask for evidence of the biblical content of this concept, which has been the very touchstone of ecumenical thinking since the Amsterdam Assembly. Their conviction that such a concept is only a new and subtler form of the classic natural law approach and for this reason does not help but 'impedes the dialogue between Scripture and daily life' and even 'tends to act as a substitute for broader and more sensitive biblical thinking about society' is a fundamental challenge. It points to the need for a clearer indication that the Responsible Society has its roots in biblical faith and does not reduce the true tension between the Gospel and the world. And the radical questions of the best

Christian minds of Africa and Asia who want support in their efforts to discover the spiritual and moral basis for Christian participation in the building of a new society, press the ecumenical movement to inquire whether its caution in speaking about how God is at work in historical social change may reflect not only certain theological difficulties but possibly an unconscious Western approach to the whole problem of social change in the new nations. It is just these kind of theological challenges which have led to the decision that the projected 1966 WCC World Conference on God, Man and Society, should focus its discussion on three questions:

1. How may Christians understand the action of God in Christ in contemporary history?

2. What may Christians expect and not expect to accomplish in the transformation of society?

3. How may Christians meet the challenge of the many radically new situations for the life and structure of the Church?

II. *The Need for a New Social Analysis, and the Means to Bring it About*

The response of many Christian laymen, however, is that the fundamental need of ecumenical social thinking is not to be met only or even primarily by new theological debates on issues which have already been the subject of a great amount of study and discussion. Theological discussions unrelated to the realities of modern complex, increasingly interdependent technical society will only convince many laymen of a certain reactionary trend in the ecumenical movement. To these laymen deeply concerned about the future of the welfare society and the problems of economic growth, the advice of Professor Bultmann is truly 'out of this world', a clear invitation to spiritual schizophrenia arising from efforts to maintain separate moral standards for the Church and the World. The criticism of the idea of the Responsible Society will seem to them pointless and absurd. They have found this concept useful precisely because it offered a means of translating ultimate biblical truth into terms meaningful for the concrete decisions of political and social life while avoiding the danger of sanctifying historical systems.

Such laymen are asking not for more theological speculation but for more incisive translation of theological and biblical ideas into the concepts and categories of the social sciences and the technical disciplines around which their life is now organized. A layman who has been active in ecumenical work argues that the great problem confronting the churches is to overcome their inability to relate their ideas to the world of political and economic affairs. He writes:

'I feel strongly that, generally speaking, in theology and corporate action the churches have not yet found the relation of the New Testament ethic to the world of concrete international responsibility. In Bonhoeffer's letters is a very revealing sentence with regard to this problem. In discussing the theology of Karl Barth he praises him highly for his dogmatics, but makes the following remark regarding his ethics: "It was not that he subsequently, as is often claimed, failed in his ethics, for his ethical observations . . . are just as significant as his dogmatic ones; it was that he gave no concrete guidance either in dogmatics or in ethics, on the non-religious interpretation of theological concepts." Some great conceptions of Christian theology in the Church of our day "remain unexplained and remote, because there is no interpretation of them". It is for this reason that I feel that the relevance of Christian faith within human conflict is uncertain in the Church today.'

Such laymen have found in ecumenical study on social questions a new and welcome opportunity to carry on a creative dialogue between theologian and layman.

They ask that the ecumenical movement take up the study of the moral issues in the change from traditional to dynamic societies, and the ethical issues raised by the contemporary concern with progress and security. Their concern is not to junk theology but to get the help of the theologian in a new theologically oriented analysis and interpretation of the changed circumstances of the contemporary life. They want to know why the churches and their institutions do not give more attention to 'the human implications of the growing scientific knowledge about man and the continuing techno-logical revolution'.

III. *The Challenge of Rapid Social Change*

It might be concluded from this description of the challenge confronting ecumenical social thinking today that the concerns of theologians and laymen will inevitably neutralize each other, producing a kind of impasse. This is not likely to happen (and not only because the theologians are in a minority). The realistic principle that lay concerns must continue to influence the direction of ecumenical study on social questions, can scarcely be challenged. The great achievement of the Oxford Conference was to draw into the ecumenical discussion the best lay minds that could be found in the Church, because it raised for the Church the questions which were before the world, and gave new vitality and appeal to the consequent thinking developed in the Conference.

Today perhaps the greatest difficulty in finding a common Christian outlook on the problems of social change does not lie in the conflicts of the theologian and the layman, but in the conflicts about social policy produced by rapid social change among laymen in all parts of the world: the tensions between youth and their elders within each country, and between youth and elders in the West and the same groups in Africa, Asia or Latin America. Rapid social change is raising new questions about Christian political and economic responsibility which we have only begun to struggle with, even in the World Council of Churches where we have given a fair amount of attention to these questions in recent years. Such conflicts will test the integrity and the representative character of the ecumenical movement in new, dangerous, and yet exciting ways.

Fortunately, at this point also the World Council can call upon certain resources which it has acquired from its experience in recent years, for example, in the long debate within the ecumenical movement about the Christian attitude toward capitalism and communism. Here was a controversy which at times has threatened to divide seriously if not wreck completely ecumenical unity (and the danger is not yet over). Without giving up its concern for either the truth or the preservation of ecumenical community, the World Council has helped its member churches to see this issue in a more universal and a more profound perspective. Those who do not recall the violent reaction of Wall Street, the American Chamber of Commerce, and the Zürich bankers to the Amsterdam Assembly statement that 'the Christian churches should reject the ideologies of both Communism and *laissez-faire* capitalism and should seek to draw men away from the false assumption that these extremes are the only alternatives', will perhaps not appreciate the extent to which the World Council has already endured the 'fires of history', of which the New Testament speaks. Mention could also be made of the struggles of the ecumenical movement to make a creative witness in the area of race and ethnic relations where the tensions have been no less severe.

We cannot however take for granted the capacity to meet the challenge of the dynamic situation in which we live, with the distrust and suspicion raised by old and new wrongs and grievances, and with the great differences in outlook which it produces today. Today and in the future, as in the past, the outcome will depend very largely on the spiritual and intellectual resources of the churches and of individual Christians, whether they can truly see what God in Christ is asking of them. There is no guarantee that we shall do what God expects of us just as there is no guarantee that we know what true faithfulness is. But there is a guarantee that God will not abandon those who earnestly seek to know and do his will, and that is finally our only hope.

The words of Visser 't Hooft in his book *None Other Gods* published in 1937 still have the ring of relevance for the situation of ecumenical social thinking today. In a chapter entitled 'Can We Stand the Strain?' he wrote:

'A Christian is then characterized, not only by the decision to follow Christ, but also by the decision to accept the renewal of life which Christ offers . . . (p. 49). That is a difficult task. And it is obvious that we cannot accomplish it alone. The whole problem of Christian ethics is basically a problem of the Christian Community. Our tragedy is that in this matter there is so very little common Christian thinking going on among us, and that we therefore act most often in a purely arbitrary way, without relation to our faith. We need a new Christian conception of the state, of war, of sex, of economics, and of many other realms of life. For the old conceptions are somehow unrelated to the problems which we face today. And only the common thought of the Christian Community can work these out for us' (pp. 53-54).

CHRISTIAN CONFESSION IN THE ASIAN REVOLUTION

M. M. Thomas

The Meaning of Confession

THE essential content of the Christian confession is that Jesus is Lord and Christ. It is a most positive act of spiritual commitment and affirmation of the Lordship of Jesus Christ over the world on the part of the believer and the community of believers; and it determines the nature of all other expressions of their being in the life of the world.

In its relation to the life of the world, such a Christian confession involves three things: *Firstly*, Christians shall worship the God and Father of our Lord Jesus Christ. *Secondly*, Christians shall worship 'none other gods'. This 'none other' denotes an act of continuous resistance of the Christian Church against the worship of idols, of gods and lords which are by nature not God, whether they be Caesar or the creations of men's religious imagination. The struggle of the early Church against Jewish legalism, the witness of the martyrs against the worship of the Roman Caesars, the protest of the Reformers against the doctrine of salvation by religious or good works, the refusal of the Church to identify Christ and his Kingdom with any secular or sacred ideology or movement of progress in history—all these, with their keynote of resistance against false gods, are integral to our understanding of the meaning of Christian confession. *Thirdly*, while resisting idolatry in all its forms, the Christian believer has the obligation to affirm that idols and offerings to idols are creatures and that when redeemed of the spirit of rebellion they have as creatures their particular place and purpose in the design of God for the world. This requires of the Church to participate in the life of the world, of persons, of social relations and institutions, and of nature, for the sake of witnessing to their divinely ordained purposes under the lordship of Christ.

In all genuine acts of Christian confession all these three aspects are present. In the New Testament approaches to idols and meats offered to idols, these truths come to light very clearly. Christians are those who 'have turned from idols to be servants of the living and true God' (I Thess. 1.9), and they should always 'be on the watch against false gods' (I John 5.21). They also 'abstain from things polluted by contact with idols' (Acts 15.20). But Christians know that 'a false god has no existence in the real world. There is no god but one.' Even if there be many lords and gods, yet for Christians 'there is one God the Father from whom all being comes, towards whom we move; and there is one Lord Jesus Christ, through whom all things came to be and we through him.' For those who know this truth, the meat offered to idols is only food and may be eaten or not eaten in good conscience. But he must respect the weaker conscience of a brother for whom it is still associated with idol-worship (I Cor. 8.9-13). The principle is clearly enunciated. 'Everything that God created is good and nothing is to be rejected when it is taken with thanksgiving, since it is hallowed by God's own word and by prayer' (I Tim. 4.4f.). While idols are to be rejected as idols, the Gospel redeems them of the spirit of perversity and consecrates them to God as good creatures.

Confession against Idolatry of the State

From the point of view of our subject perhaps it is more relevant to illustrate the meaning of Christian confession in relation to the experience of the Church, in relation to the Caesars, in the periods of the New Testament and after it. The study *Christ and the Caesars* by E. Stauffer has shown how the Church witnessed to the Kings of kings, and the one Redeemer by refusing to surrender to the demands of Caesars for worship. The Book of Revelation itself is a standing testimony to this act of confession. Christians were prevented by their conscience from entering military and civil service, because these services were integrated with Caesar-worship. At the same time, Romans 13 with its affirmation of the divine institution of the State and its divinely ordained function of promoting justice stands as an essential part of the Christian confession. The Christian refusal to sacrifice to Caesar and the Christian acceptance of the service which the State is called to render to mankind under God are not antithetical, but of the same piece, and must be considered together in understanding the meaning of Christian confession. In fact, the history of the witness of martyrs of the Roman period gives ample evidence that theirs was not a political but a religious opposition and that politically they saw the Roman State as rendering a divine service.

The history of the Confessing Church in Germany during the days of Hitler has had a decisive influence in our day in defining Christian confession. Cullmann in his study of the *State in the New Testament* has a passage where he defines the difference between the Caesarism of Rome and the Hitlerism of Germany. Caesarism, while demanding Caesar-worship as a test of a citizen's loyalty to it, nevertheless was sensitive to the moral order in its promotion of legal and political justice. Hitlerism not only demanded total loyalty in adoration and ideology but also carried its totalitarianism to the extent of integrating the concepts and practice of law and politics with the Nazi ideology and its repudiation of any moral reality transcending the State. For this reason, the Christian confession of the Lordship of Christ had to express the spiritual resistance against the idolatry of Hitlerism in two forms—one religious resistance against its attempt to define God, Christ and the Church in Nazi ideological terms, and the other political non-co-operation and resistance to Hitler's political order which itself had become institutionalized idolatry. But it must be noted that the political non-co-operation and resistance to Hitler's political order on the part of the confessing Christians was never total in the first place; they discriminated between those laws and acts of State which were clearly integrated with Nazi ideology and those which could be conceived of as coming within the normal divinely ordained services of government. The political resistance became total only with the Second World War; and in the case of martyrs like Dietrich Bonhoeffer who played a part in the plan (which failed) to overthrow Hitler, such clear political resistance to Hitler in political terms was based on their conviction that the Hitler-State *in toto* was a repudiation of the divinely instituted servant-state and has to be totally replaced by one which conformed to it.

The different forms of Christian confession in relation to Caesarism and Hitlerism were based on a common understanding of the meaning of confession, namely (1) total allegiance to the revelation in Christ in adoration and faith, (2) total resistance to any attempt of State or Church to live by any other revelation about the ultimate meaning of life and (3) discerning approach to the political, legal and administrative services of the State. This last may result in active co-operation, non-co-operation, relative resistance or total resistance depending upon two questions: (a) What institutions and acts of State are totally integrated with and expressive of idolatrous worship repudiating God in Christ? and (b) What institutions are fulfilling the divine ordinance of the State as servant of men and justice in society?

One of the unfortunate results of identifying the pattern of the Confessing Church in Germany as the pattern of all Christian confession in relation to the modern state has been the too easy assumption found even among some of the good professors of Christian social ethics, that confession in modern states which are inspired by anti-Christian or totalitarian ideologies should involve not only spiritual resistance but invariably also political resistance. There is in this a confusion of spiritual resistance with political resistance. Spiritual resistance can and should go with different political stances, ranging from constructive participation to active political resistance depending on how far we are dealing with institutionalized idolatry even in political and civil order, and how far political and civil institutions serve the ends of justice.

Confession of Participation

No doubt in situations where idolatry of nation, class or race or other secular religious ideology has become fully institutionalized in a totally closed state and society, the path of confession is clearly and simply resistance and suffering. There is no ambiguity about the path; and it has a certain heroism of martyrdom about it. For this reason, many people consider such a situation as the ideal for Christians to be in. Whether ideal or not, it is not the situation that is given to us in Asia and Africa today.

My main concern in this essay is with the implications of Christian confession in the revolutions of Asia and Africa, which are under the inspiration of the idea of modern nationalism. The proposition I would like to present is that Christian confession in the national revolutions of Asia and Africa should mean the spiritual resistance to ideological or institutional idolatry within the context of an active constructive participation in the struggle for national independence and nation-building.

If there was an institutional integration of culture, society and state with other gods in Africa and Asia, it was in the traditional culture, whether of tribe, of caste or of communal groupings. In the face of the rigidity of this integration of the

163

traditional cultures and societies with other religious cults, the modern missionary movement developed a pattern of confession, which involved both refusal to worship the old gods and withdrawal from participation in the culture and society which were part and parcel of that worship. The withdrawal may have been into the mission compound and its alien culture so that probably the confession did not always point to Christ only but to a Christ confused with western culture. This was its weakness. Nevertheless it was a pattern of witness in the face of cultures integrated with other gods. To-day, however, what we are facing in Africa and Asia is the breakdown of this traditional integration between religion and cultural institutions through the impact of the Gospel, and the other gods of the West, as well as the ideal and material goods of Western culture. At the levels of state, society and culture, Africa and Asia are seeking both a renewal and a new synthesis transcending the traditional and the Western. In such a situation, there is a great deal of uncertainty about the goals towards which they should move as well as the means to achieve them. There are no doubt strong tendencies to ideological total-itarianism based on the traditional gods or the modern secular gods in the revolution, as evidenced by the militant revival of the traditional religions in some parts of Africa and Asia, and the hold of Communism in others. And in some countries, one or other of such totalitarian ideologies may appear to have come to control the shape of things. But these must be con-sidered as no more than tentative experiments on the part of the people seeking renewal of their political, social and cultural institutions. The uncertainty about the pattern of the new life they aspire to and the instruments of its realization remain true even in those countries. Probably the gods themselves appear more militant than usual in these areas precisely because they are not sure of their staying power. Most certainly the strength of the idea of the secular State in some countries, and the rule by the military junta in others, point to the fact that the revolution in Africa and Asia has not found its final shape one way or the other. In this new situation which the Asian churches face, spiritual resistance to the false gods (either strong at present or emerging to strength) requires their affirmation of solidarity with the new aspirations and hopes of their peoples and an active partnership with them in their search for and experiments in new patterns of living. For the people need to be convinced that they can have the creaturely goods and social justice which they aspire to as creatures without making them the gods of their worship. In the act of Christian confession in Asian and African countries today, there is need not only for proclaiming the one Lord, and for resisting the claims of other lords, but also for emphasizing that the new human values which the people seek can be seen, realized and maintained in their essential humanity only as good gifts of God within the context of God's design in Christ for all men. This, however, is an emphasis which can be communicated only in solidarity with and partnership in the people's struggles for these values. That is why the Christian concern for the proper dignity of man and his creaturely values is integral to the Christian confession today, at least in the newly emerging nations.

No doubt, in the face of the renascent traditional religions and modern secular ideologies with their militant anti-Christian stance, the temptation for Christians to delude themselves as being called for a simple martyr's heroism is very strong at certain times and places. But it must be rejected as temptation until the anti-Christian forces have taken total control of the institutions of culture leaving no room for Christian – non-Christian partnership in common struggle for order, freedom and justice except on the basis of apostasy. In no country in Asia or Africa has such a general situation arisen. There may be critical situations for particular persons or churches and they must face it. Every anti-church idea or movement should not be interpreted as opposed to the God in Christ. Perhaps it may be the voice of God judging the false gods within the life of the Church; and judgment should begin with the house of God. And a Church repentant and justified by faith (and not by its past works) can discriminate between what is of Christ and what of the anti-Christ even in the anti-church urges within the revolution, and may even be able to help the revolutionary leaders to make that discrimination. This may help pave the way for Christian partnership in society at a new human level. This does not mean the Asian revolution cannot or will not become institutionalized opposition to Jesus Christ himself. It may. But it has not yet so become. Whatever awaits the churches in these lands in the future, we are called today to partnership and participation in the struggle for the true ends of the revolution within the design of God for man's creaturely existence.

Christ as Lord and Redeemer of the Revolution

The assumption behind this whole approach is that the present revolution in Africa and Asia has in it the promise of God for a fuller and real human life for men; that it is possible for faith to discern it in the light of the revelation of the True Man Jesus Christ; and that this insight of faith may be shared however partially by men of other faiths and no faith within a partnership of thought and action. These no doubt are big assumptions. But they seem to be corroborated by the experience of the Church.

What then are some of the human aspirations within the revolution which the Church needs to affirm in its confession of the Lordship of Christ over his creation?

1. The revolution contains within it man's search for freedom as the power and responsibility to create. The increasing mastery of nature in science and industry, as well as the creation of new dynamic forms of community in the place of the old static social structures, represent the new urges of Asian and African men to exercise creativity which has been released. If there is a great deal of atheism and dogmatic secularism

among the leaders of the revolutionary struggles of Asia and Africa, part of this must be interpreted as a protest against the ideas of God and the practice of religious control of culture which left no room for man's creativeness.

2. The revolution is marked by a new sense of self-awareness which is expressed in the demand for self-determination and self-development. The national struggle for freedom is a movement expressing the nation's self-awareness. In the process of nation-building, all individuals and traditional groups are being awakened to a similar sense of selfhood and its rights. This search for responsible selfhood indicates the discovery of an essential element of man's humanness. The self's knowledge of itself and of other selves by persons and groups of persons does create more problems of alienation and conflict than before. But alienation and reconciliation, hell and heaven, are meaningful terms and real possibilities only to those who know themselves to be responsible selves. This self-knowledge is undoubtedly an aspect of the growth of man's humanity.

3. Through the revolution the people are seeking more humane forms of social justice and community than they ever knew before. They are rejecting traditional collectivism with its suppression of individuality and equality. What the out-castes, who are on the lowest rung of the traditional hierarchy, revolt against most is paternalism, which reduced persons to functions and personalized the areas of life which ought to be treated impersonally in terms of law. The revolution represents the search of people for a pattern of community in which both law and love are creatively related, that is for the social conditions of men's humanity.

4. Through the revolution the people are seeing history as the area of the fulfilment of their human destiny. The world view of resignation, the fatalism of the static patterns of living and the cyclic conceptions of history are giving way to the dynamic of purposive history moving towards goals. The

goals may be misconceived or even missed. This brings often for the first time the sense of the tragic element into the picture. The new sense of historical dynamism, even if it brings tragedy and despair, opens up a higher dimension of human existence for the people.

When we say that the Revolution has within it the promise of the growth of these elements of man's essential humanity, it does not mean that we return to a utopian interpretation of history or an out-dated idea of progress. It is necessary to reiterate that the vision of heaven brings hell nearer. The new awareness of men of their deeper spiritual humanity has brought into being new spiritual powers of evil, which may well emerge victorious. The newly-formed creativeness may tempt man to elevate himself to the position of the Creator and to refuse to acknowledge a given moral reality transcending himself. And this may lead his creativeness into morally destructive channels. Self-discovery often leads to self-centredness expressing itself in the self-seeking of man both for power and interests resulting in new forms of exploitation; or it may lead to an endless search for moral self-justification resulting in either frustration or ideological fanaticism. The passion for freedom and justice may replace the traditional collectivism either by the anarchy of individualism or the ruthless tyranny of an impersonal mass-society. The sense of history and historical vocation may tempt the nation or some class or other group within it, to set themselves up as a new Messiah to save mankind and bring history to fulfilment. This rather simple and utopian false messianism might well then be the precursor or the Grand Inquisitor of ideological totalitarianism and coercive tyranny.

And as a matter of fact, all these new evils are at work in the revolution in Africa and Asia, so that there is nothing inevitable about the fulfilment of the human aspirations behind the revolutionary ferment; and there is a high degree of possibility that they may be betrayed from within. This means that the

Church's affirmation of Christ's promise in the revolution of a fuller human life for people cannot be made in isolation from her witness to the offer of his victory over principalities and powers through his Cross and Resurrection, and the offer of his Kingdom and his New Humanity within the revolution itself. There can be no true humanism without the evangel. In our world, the confession of Christ and the defence of man, his universal rights and the oneness of mankind, have in several critical times been seen as integral to each other. The Barmen Declaration in Germany, the church struggle in South Africa, and the sit-in-strikes in the U.S.A.—they have shown that, when humanitarians and liberal humanists and even Christian churches have found themselves unable to resist the demonic powers of statism and racism, the confession of faith in Christ as the only Lord of the world and the Church did provide the resistance. But this insight about the vital relation between the Gospel and humanism must find expression in the normal obligations of Christian citizenship in the revolutions of Africa and Asia today. Already many are becoming conscious of the depths of spiritual corruption and demoralization inherent in the revolution and of the inevitability of compromise with them in order to check them and achieve a measure of order, freedom and justice. In such a situation there is the possibility of a universal loss of nerve. And only those who live by faith in Christ's Resurrection in history and by hope in the coming of Christ beyond the appearance of the Anti-Christ at the end (and/or those who share the insights of such faith and hope) can sustain the revolution in its struggle for humane institutions of politics, society and culture. It is this that makes exercise of Christian citizenship in Asia and Africa today a real act of Christian confession.

In conclusion, let me quote a passage from Dr Visser 't Hooft, to whom the writers in this volume of essays owe a great deal. Speaking at the New Delhi Assembly of the World Council of Churches, he said 'We are called to glorify God in the Church.

We are equally called to glorify him in the world. For, however rebellious that world has become, it is destined to be the theatre of his glory.' Through the last half-century of ecumenism, we have learned that the Church is a constitutive element of the Gospel of Jesus Christ. We are now learning in a new way that the world, as 'destined to be the theatre of his glory' is equally, if not more, integral to the Gospel.

LAY REFLECTIONS ON OIKOUMENE

Kathleen Bliss

IN a large room desks are set out. Notices divide them into members, substitutes, fraternal delegates, observers. Wires trail across the floor from translators' desks labelled French, German, Russian, to microphones and loudspeakers. Stacks of duplicated documents stand ready. Any international gathering anywhere in the world might be imminent, but for one fact. Behind the dais hangs a great blue backcloth and on it floats the familiar white ship with cross as mast: below the ship the decorous waves, above it the word OIKOUMENE.

A meeting of the Central Committee of the World Council of Churches affords its members eight days for intermittent contemplation of this symbol, and few organizations have been blessed with a symbol that wears so well, with its combination of simplicity and mystery. Here is the ship of the Church, not as our churches seem to be, loaded with devices for propelling them along and steering them in this or that direction. There is nothing to catch the wind, nothing to use the tide: simply the cross and commitment to the waves. The Church is given to the world, and the tides which carry it are God's tides, but they flow through the world under the cross. But *these* waves with their neatly structured symmetry are too decorous by half to remind us of the Psalmist's connection between the violence of the sea and the tumult of the people flung against the Ark of the Lord and threatening to engulf it.

But the feature of the symbol most worthy of contemplation is surely the word *oikoumene*. How fortunate is the World Council of Churches not to have put its own name to what has become so widely identified as its own sign. Taking a very ancient symbol of the Christian Church, it has kept also a very ancient word. It is salutary for committees in particular to remember that neither they nor the organization they represent are the *oikoumene* which can mean nothing less than the whole Church in the whole world. The ecumenical movement is other than, and greater than, the institutions and organizations which have become its chief expression. The large volume of the *History* of the ecumenical movement is a dangerous volume if to any reader it seems to indicate that the story reaches its end or even its climax with the foundation of the World Council of Churches. This event is not an arrival at a destination: it is a point on a long, long journey, a wayside station where energies are replenished, maps consulted, and the journey taken up with new companions and new energies. Every Christian belongs in the ecumenical movement who, looking beyond the narrow confines of his parish or group, nation or tribe, sees and greets as a brother on the journey another man, another church, another co-operator in a new task, another seeker of the unity of the Church in Christ its Head. Every impulse belongs to the ecumenical movement which carries the Church out into the world, whether to the ends of the earth to preach the Gospel and heal the sick, or to the world physically so near and yet in other ways so far, the world of a technical civilization operating under impulses which seem to allow little place for the Church as institution or the Gospel as inspiring faith.

The ecumenical movement—the search for the recovery, first as a vision, a driving concept in church life, and then as a reality, of the whole Church in the whole world—has been

carried forward on the shoulders of great men: many of them
have been spiritual and intellectual giants. Their story has often
been written and credit given also to the innumerable other
men and women whose devotion and sacrifice and plain hard
work contributed so much to the whole. But the birth and
growth of ideas is more subtle than historians and biographers
sometimes allow. If we have learned from Martin Buber and
his exponents to understand the statement that the truth is not
in the I or in the Thou but between the I and the Thou, then
we would expect that the birth of ideas is generated by what
we as Christians would unquestionably call the work of the
Holy Spirit operating between men. Precisely because the
ecumenical movement has brought men from the structures of
their own churches and as representatives of their churches into
a free association with no hierarchy or authority, no precedents
or rules (beyond those of procedure), its driving force has had
to be the free engagement of minds and spirits. The Roman
Catholic observer who said of the ecumenical movement 'We
have the authority of the undivided Church: but you know
one another' was saying something more profound than
perhaps he meant: for 'knowing', in Old Testament parlance,
is a way of begetting: it is creative, not sterile; and the true
begetting of the ecumenical movement has been a begetting
not of institutions but of ideas.

It may be that we are at a critical turning point now on our
ecumenical journey. Confronted with the stacks of blue paper,
each piece of which represents the work of another committee
or perhaps even of several in succession, the Central Committee
may insensibly lapse into the role of a relater of institutions.
So the member sits at his desk and asks 'To what committee
or office letter-box in my church do I direct this piece of paper
or that?' He could so easily give up the struggle to engage with
ideas because the sheer pressure of quantity is too great. God
forbid that we should be the instruments of killing the
ecumenical movement by ossifying ideas and entombing them

in paper and crushing those who might be the future begetters with the sheer weight of our own whited sepulchres! Our question therefore is: How can we keep the ecumenical movement in control of its institutions? How can we maintain or create the conditions in which, through communication of mind to mind and spirit to spirit, ideas have their birth and grow over widening circles of the Church's life? That is a question to which time and thought has to be given, but perhaps a small contribution to that thinking can be made by an attempt to trace the history of one ecumenical idea—the vocation and ministry of the laity.

What follows is not in the strict sense of the word a history; there will be no references and learned footnotes. But as I have read the histories of the various movements which have flowed together in the present ecumenical movement, and the biographies of many of its leading figures, and delved into the many volumes of the many reports of many of the great conferences, and have, indeed, taken part in not a few, I recognize by sympathy rather than by scholarship the ancestors of the ideas with which I have been privileged to work in partnership with J. H. Oldham in the Christian Frontier Council, and in other expressions of the ecumenical effort, to discover and fulfil the vocation and the ministry of the laity in the world. The story looks to me something like this.

The ecumenical movement as we know it had its origins in the impulses of the Evangelical revival. This revival imparted to those who were touched by it not docile piety but the freedom and authority and new obligation to act and speak as under the direct, uninterrupted control of the Spirit of God. The Evangelical revival was in curious ways the spiritual counterpart of the Enlightenment. As the Enlightenment set free the human mind to pursue knowledge unhampered by the strait-jacket of formalized and institutionalized thought, so also the Evangelical revival gave men not just a subjective religious experience, but a sudden apprehension of the whole

world in a different way. This is a constituent in many con-
versions. All sorts of things seemed possible. It touched men of
learning and authority, and practical men working with their
hands, with the same sense of freedom to respond and act,
passing like a contagion from one to another. Out of this were
born the lay movements of the nineteenth century and the
conventions and the student camps.

It is astonishing to see the speed with which the fire leapt
from country to country, continent to continent, carried often
by laymen whom nobody now remembers. These lay movements provided for Christian men and women the outlet for
this Evangelical fervour in mission and service. While missionary expansion thrust out into the non-Christian world, the
lay movements spread not only into the whole of the mainly
Protestant West, but significantly into South America and into
the world of Orthodoxy in Russia, the Balkans and the near
East. While, at times and in places, the lay movements seemed to
provide for some of their members a broad road from the
churches to a kind of undenominationalism which left the
churches just where they were in relation to one another, and
thence by declining stages to a pale shadow of Christian belief
and action, they also provided precisely the opposite, namely a
standing-ground from which men and women could see the
Church in a new light and work to make the actual churches
become what this vision disclosed. It is extremely difficult to
think that John R. Mott could have done the things he did if
he had been anything other than a layman.

Profoundly influenced, like J. H. Oldham and many others
of the ecumenical pioneers, by the evangelism of Dwight L.
Moody and his associates, Mott decided to give his life, in his
own words, 'to the service of Jesus'. Signing the Princeton
Pledge, which was the forerunner of the missionary commitment of the Student Volunteer Missionary Union, he put
without facetiousness or indecision in the space labelled
'Chosen field of service' 'The world'. It was as a YMCA

secretary,[1] working especially among the 'student Y's' already established and bringing new ones into being, that Mott made that encounter with the Orthodox which is of such extreme importance to the later development of the ecumenical movement. Untrained in theology, and never suffering from the disease of being the parson *manqué* which prevents so many lay people from seeing and pursuing the fullness of their lay vocation in freedom, Mott, from his standing-ground in the YMCA, could see the importance of helping the Orthodox to be themselves and to come into relation with others. Mott was by common consent the chief founder of the World's Student Christian Federation in 1895, and served it as secretary and then as chairman (giving almost his whole time to it) from that date till 1928. During this period he and the secretaries of the national movements associated with the WSCF created relationship between the members of different churches who came into those movements totally different from the old undenominationalism of half a century before. This new ecumenical fellowship was based on the principle of bringing everything into the encounter instead of leaving every disagreement out. Thus Bishop Gore who, with Tissington Tatlow, played so important a role in getting the Anglo-Catholic wing of the Church of England at Edinburgh in 1910, could write to the SPG that in the Student Christian Movement there was to be found something quite different from the undenominationalism and the possible compromise of principle which they feared. To bring and hold together disagreeing opposites was part of Mott's genius. The devotion, fire and

[1] Writing of his time as YMCA secretary to students in Lahore J. H. Oldham says: 'So far as I know Mott had nothing to do directly with this appointment. Indirectly he probably may have had a good deal. He had already sent out hand-picked very able Americans to man the YMCA's in Bombay, Madras and Calcutta, as well as Brockman to China—probably the most influential foreigner in China in any capacity—and Galen Fisher, also outstanding, to Japan. . . . I of course, saw a good deal of his able lieutenants in India.'

missionary commitment which made him not only the organizer but the powerful evangelist that he was came to him from the Evangelical revival. But he acquired from his personal friendships with many great churchmen a spiritual awareness of the essential marks of the Church. Mott's contribution to the emergence of the ecumenical perception of the role of the laity was, in my view, that he was one of the main creators of the cradle in which it could be born, for he was the leader of a company of men who held the emphasis on personal commitment and individual initiative characteristic of the Evangelical revival, the lay movements and the missionary movements, in the closest possible proximity with the catholicity and order of the unbroken tradition of Christendom, which was the carrier of so much of the concept of *oikoumene* from the earliest centuries across a great leap of time to the present day. The ecumenical emphasis on the laity calls on the individual layman to see the world as the place where God wills him to live out his faith, and on the churches to recognize the laity as the Church in the world and to equip them for their task. In no aspect of ecumenical endeavour do 'evangelical' and 'catholic' more greatly need one another.

The great contribution of Edinburgh 1910 to the ecumenical idea which we are here pursuing was that it moved out of the realm of missionary demonstration designed merely to elicit interest and support (which all previous missionary conferences had been) into the realm of planning by responsible church leaders of the missionary strategy of the Church. Mott, as chairman of the preparatory commissions, and Oldham, appointed secretary to the conference two years before it took place, worked to put into leading positions in the conference men who had never co-operated before, and successfully engaged them in an enterprise which did more than anything else to make mission and outreach a part of the essential thinking of the leaders of the Church. True, the constituent bodies were missionary societies, but the executive committee in

Britain (for example) appointed a delegation which included the archbishops and seven diocesan bishops, the moderators or presidents of the Church of Scotland and all the Free Churches. Continental and American churches also sent leading church-men—hardly a free-lance body of missionary enthusiasts! While so many forces were tending to isolate the Church, as was clearly described in a Church of England report of 1902 on the role of the laity, the missionary movement was not only itself going out into the world, but was turning the eyes of the Church's chief leaders towards that *oikoumene* which is by its original use 'the inhabited world'.

The official aim of the Edinburgh conference was 'to consider missionary problems in relation to the non-Christian world'. Hidden in this was the assumption that there was a Christian world—the West—and outside it in Asia and Africa a non-Christian world occupied by other religions. Hence the omission of the whole sub-continent of South America from Edinburgh's purview. One of the commissions was called 'Unoccupied fields', which meant 'geographical areas where the Gospel has not yet been preached'. The continuation committee and later the International Missionary Council provided, it is true, a means of consultation and joint action, and it is in this light that they are usually seen as new ecumenical achievements. But, equally important, they provided a means of continual study of the relationships between the missionary enterprise and aspects of the developing life of the countries in which that enterprise was carried on. Missions were deeply committed both to education and to medical work. This was an outreach of the work of the Church which brought with it a host of problems which in the IMC were objectively studied by a series of commissions and enquiries on which distinguished educators served along with men like Tom Jones who was shaping the social policies of Britain. It became customary to listen to the advice of the lay expert and not to rely solely on the collective wisdom or unwisdom of committees.

The Jerusalem meeting of the IMC in 1928 has, in my view, been sadly underestimated in the total assessment of ecumenical development. It was a meeting at which divisions became apparent. The missionary drive had come largely from the Evangelical revival. The heart of it was still the personal call and commitment of the individual missionary, but Jerusalem showed how difficult it was and would be to hold those powerful impulses always in that engagement with the Church to which Mott and others had brought it. There were criticisms that the proposal to study social questions by setting up a department for Social and Industrial Research meant a turning away from the priority of preaching the Gospel. In vain was it argued that such a study prepared the way for more effective preaching of the Gospel.

Even greater was the division about the central topic of the meeting, which was 'The Christian Message'. Although the meeting itself accepted in complete agreement the statement on 'the Christian Message', with its key sentence 'Our message is Jesus Christ', afterwards there were some accusations of papering over the divisions with fine words. On the one hand were those who were prepared to recognize in other religions a truth and a goodness not totally irreconcilable with the Gospel; on the other hand stood those who saw in the Gospel something so new and so radical, so entirely dependent upon revelation, that at no point could there be any contact with other religions and other ways. The force and power of Karl Barth's thought served to heighten the tension and later to deepen thought on both sides. We saw the tension demonstrated at New Delhi, but then there also came into the open, not only in connection with the argument whether God was or was not at work in other religions, a strong and clear challenge to believing that Christ is at work in *all* his world. There are marked parallels between the role of the missionary in a non-Christian culture and the layman in the secular structures of the modern world, and the theological discussion of the work of

Christ in the world of non-Christian religions is highly relevant
to a discussion of the work of Christ in a secularized society.

The Jerusalem conference was followed up by an unprecedented amount of theological discussion. Not only were
groups of theologians called together in different countries by
the IMC, but the quality of the Jerusalem statement itself made
it a document to be discussed in many a theological college and
seminary where it fell into a relevant context of discussion
about the formulation of the Christian message in the modern
world.

Jerusalem had no commission on 'Unoccupied fields', but
one could almost say that its place was taken by a discussion on
secularism. Certain members of the staff, especially William
Paton, wanted secularism to figure among the 'other religions'
with which the Christian mission had to do. A paper by Rufus
Jones, an American Quaker and something of a mystic, called
'Secular civilizations and the Christian task', described the rise
and spread throughout the world of a new civilization based on
science and technology, and the growth of an attitude of mind
which set out to master the world of nature for human ends
without any reference to a supernatural sanction. The discussion which took place at Jerusalem contained, of course, some
castigations of materialism. But other voices bade the Church
listen and learn. Canon Oliver Quick, for example, spoke of
the chastening influence on the Church of having 'to interpret
self-sacrifice intellectually' which meant, he said, 'fearless
willingness to face the weather of fact', and Canon Charles
Raven, himself a distinguished scientist, said: 'Secular civilization has provided a satisfying opportunity for personal
development, not only in the pursuit of truth, but also in the
providing of outlets for activities which supply all the values
which religion was accustomed to provide. . . . Our problem
is to find how Christianity can baptize the new learning and
the new social order with the spirit of Christ.'

The tensions at Jerusalem were part of the agonies of realizing that 'the world', for Christian mission, was something more than a geographical term. The debate on secularism showed that the field of mission is also a universal culture, one created by, and present in, the West. The mission, therefore, is everywhere: but what of the message? Granted that it is Jesus Christ, how does the Church speak of him to those who are being rapidly moved out of the context of any religion? To return to the symbol of the ship: what is the job of the evangelist? To let down the net and draw the fish into the ship, or are there moments when, casting his cloak about him, he must throw himself into the water and swim towards the Lord who is standing on the shore? I wonder whether there is any significance in the fact that on both occasions when an apostle in the gospel narrative so leaps from the boat and commits himself to the waves, it is Peter, *the* apostle of the Church?

After the Jerusalem meeting Oldham (who had not been present because, as the result of his work with governments on behalf of the IMC, he was serving on a Government Commission in East Africa) was, in relation to this idea of the secular civilization, almost as a man possessed. It filled his thoughts for many months and at the next IMC committee (in July, 1929) he presented a paper later published under the title 'The New Christian Adventure'. In this paper he drew a balanced and very telling picture of the characteristic features of secular civilization. 'It is', he wrote, 'no academic theory or speculative philosophy. It is intimately associated with the creative forces of the modern world. It is not a body of traditional beliefs, to which men pay an outward and respectful homage while their real interests lie elsewhere. What we have to reckon with is the assumptions underlying and bound up with the living forces which are here and now building up the world in which we live.' To men who had come powerfully under the influence of these ideas (and they were being spread widely by education) a personal God seemed an irrelevance, even a hindrance: with the loss of belief in a personal God 'goes the abandonment of belief in a divine purpose for the world, in any cosmic significance of human life and conduct, in personal immortality, in prayer and worship, and in the providential ordering of the life of individuals and of society. It needs but little reflection to realize how immense are the spiritual values which thus disappear from human life.' He recognized too the effect of secular civilization on men still over-committed to the Church and the Christian faith. 'We cannot have a world-conquering Christianity, so long as the Christian mind is divided against itself, and men try to keep their belief in God in a compartment of their mind, while with the rest of their nature they share in the activities of a society based on assumptions that leave no place for him. . . . The books that are needed to answer the questions in men's minds are not being produced in sufficient numbers nor of sufficient quality. . . . There is a great task to be undertaken by Christian thinkers—not as an isolated effort but as an integral part of a new adventure of life and of a deepening of spiritual experience on the part of the whole Church.' 'The New Christian Adventure' ends with an appeal to the IMC. 'The International Missionary Council is in a sense the trustee of the idea of the world mission of Christianity. With the knowledge we have of the world situation we want to approach new groups—not only Christian scholars and theologians, but laymen. . . . We do not want to ask merely or primarily for their support of the organized missionary movement. Our appeal is wider than that. We want to say to them, "This, as we understand it, is the world situation with which Christianity is faced. How, in your own distinctive sphere, can you help to meet it?"'

Followers of the present ecumenical discussion of the role of the laity will recognize many characteristic features in this document written nearly a quarter of a century ago. But there are still many churches and countries where what the Christian is doing in 'his distinctive sphere' as schoolmaster or trade unionist is not thought of in terms of mission, and where the idea of asking the layman to contribute out of his own lay experience in the world to the thinking of the Church about its task is scarcely born.

'The New Christian Adventure' had a wide circulation in the United States and in Germany. Some of those who had been at Jerusalem went away and did just what Oldham pleaded for; Charles Raven, for example, and Karl Heim of Germany. It was unquestionably this pre-occupation of Oldham's which led George Bell, the Bishop of Chichester and chairman of the Universal Council for Life and Work, to invite Oldham to the Council's next meeting, held at Fanø, where he was at once made chairman of the research department and effectively, from that moment, the architect of the Oxford conference on Church, Community and State.

It was the Oxford conference which began to spell out the role of the laity as the spearhead of the Church's mission in a world of secularized ideas and secular institutions. Oldham, in the preparatory volume for Oxford, described the main task of the conference thus: 'If the Christian faith is in the present and future to bring about changes as it has done in the past in the thought, habits and practices of society, it can only do this through being the living, working faith of multitudes of lay men and women conducting the ordinary affairs of life. . . . We stand before a great historic task: the task of restoring the lost unity between worship and work.' Many prophets had spoken these last words: the achievement of Oxford was to begin to spell out their meaning in specific areas of the life of community and state.

After Oxford Oldham was engaged in two main activities. He was mainly responsible for drawing together a council in Great Britain which took its name from one of the commissions of the Oxford Conference and was called the 'Council on the Christian Faith and the Common Life'. Its small membership contained the Archbishops of Canterbury and York (Lang and Temple), and the heads of the English Free Churches. These

were balanced by an equal number of laymen, most of whom
had taken an important part at Oxford. They included Sir
Walter Moberly, Sir Fred Clarke, R. H. Tawney, T. S. Eliot,
and Mr Henry Brook. They addressed themselves mainly to the
practical question as to where the churches should first turn
their efforts to get the insights of Oxford effectively engaged
with some section of the life of community and state. They
decided on education and drew up a memorandum on educa-
tional advance which in many respects foreshadowed the 1944
Education Act.

The Council also decided to have its own organ and in
October 1939, in the first weeks of the war, the *Christian
Newsletter* appeared under Oldham's editorship and continued
publication, at first weekly and then fortnightly, throughout
the war. The *Newsletter*, small in compass and easily read in the
pressures of war, circulated not only among allies and neutrals,
but found its way through the offices of the embryo World
Council in Geneva (into which the Universal Council of Life
and Work had voluntarily dissolved itself) into enemy
territory. It continued the discussions of Oxford. Thus it held
together theological thinking about the Church and its
mission, and the practical expertise of Christian laymen who
knew the world in which that mission had to operate.

After a short life which exemplified the difficulties of
managing a team of archbishops and outstanding laymen (as a
letter from R. H. Tawney apologizing for 'treading on the
Archbishop's corns—I had no idea they were tender about
church schools' clearly showed) the Council on the Christian
Faith and the Common Life had voluntarily dissolved in order
to make way on the one hand for the more officially ecclesiastical set-up of the British Council of Churches, and on the
other for a lay adventure which would, as Oldham said, 'tunnel
at the same problems from the other end,' i.e. the end of the
layman in the world. This was the Christian Frontier Council,
whose organ the *Newsletter* then became.

Oldham's other activity between Oxford and shortly after the end of the war was less well-known but probably more influential. This was called 'The Moot'. It was a group of a dozen distinguished theologians, philosophers, educators and scientists. It did nothing but meet. It never produced a corporate statement, still less a corporate book. Its members included at various times John Baillie, Alec Vidler, Sir Hector Hetherington (Principal of Glasgow University), Sir Walter Moberly (Chairman of the University Grants Committee), Sir Fred Clarke, Karl Mannheim, the sociologist, Michael Polanyi, T. S. Eliot, Donald Mackinnon, H. A. Hodges, and John Middleton Murry. 'It was', said John Baillie, 'the greatest formative influence in fifteen years of my life.' Circulating to one another chapters of projected books and papers on key ideas at which they were working, and discussing these, first personally with Oldham and then corporately in the quarterly weekend meetings of the group, the members of the Moot became an intellectual Christian fraternity, full of tension, even of irritation, but full of life. Its records, kept by Professor Eric Fenn, who had been one of the Oxford secretaries, showed a continuous development of key ideas in the working out of the interconnection between the Christian faith and some of the dominant ideas of our time in the realms of philosophy and science.

The decision to set up a 'department on the laity' followed logically from the meetings of a special commission and section respectively at Amsterdam and at Evanston. In its short life this department has succeeded in carrying its theological reflection on the vocation and ministry of the laity deep into the membership of many of the churches, thanks in large measure to an exemplary clarity and brevity of statement. But as ideas spread more widely they usually lose depth and there is need for constant replenishment of the content of the 'lay idea' if we are not to be landed with a naïve 'laicism' quite as objectionable as the 'clericalism' it is now fashionable to deplore.

The problem of size may defeat the World Council of Churches in its laudable endeavours to get an adequate number of lay men and women on to its central representative bodies. Increases of membership will mean cuts in the size of delegations and an increase of those one and two member delegations which are almost always (inescapably) clerical. But the presence of the essential 'lay aspect' of the Church does not depend mechanically on the substitution of soft collars for dog collars at meetings. It depends on the steady determination of the churches (including not least the clergy) to live by the vision of the Church as the community of Christ interpenetrating the life of the world as the bearer of that Gospel whose fruit is to make 'a new creation' and render man fit for communion with God and community with other men. Far from relegating worship to the periphery, this vision brings worship to the centre. The importance of the liturgical movement for this growing awareness of the 'lay character' of the Church's being in the world, has only just begun to be explored. The importance of the Orthodox is not just that they have lay theologians and lay movements of an exciting kind, but that in ways the West finds hard to understand their worship has retained the place of the laity as active participants in the worship of a community transcending all differences, even that of time.

This little essay has perhaps shown that ideas develop by starting in one place or group and springing to another. We cannot departmentalize them. As the organizational centre of the ecumenical movement grows in size and in pressure of work it needs an increased, not a diminished, belief that it is not the *oikoumene*. The Spirit blows where it wills in the whole Church and the whole world and to catch the whisper of its breathing needs stillness at the heart of our activity.

THE LAITY: ITS GIFTS
AND MINISTRY

H. R. Weber

THE ecumenical movement and the World Council of Churches were once described by Dr W. A. Visser 't Hooft as 'essentially an attempt to manifest the economy of the *charismata*. Its purpose is to bring the churches in such vital spiritual relations with each other that they joyfully discover how much they have to receive from each other and humbly prepare to use their own spiritual gifts for the cause of the Church in the whole world.'[1]

In yet another way the ecumenical movement is manifesting today the economy of the charismata: in its reaffirmation of the ministry of the laity. Usually the charismata are mentioned in connection with the origin, authority and function of ordained ministers who have been set apart within God's people for a special ministry.[2] But equally important is the far less studied

[1] W. A. Visser 't Hooft, 'The Economy of the Charismata and the Ecumenical Movement', in *Paulus-Hellas-Oikumene: an ecumenical symposium* (published by the Student Christian Association of Greece, Athens 1951), p. 192.

[2] There is an ever-growing literature on the order and ministry of the New Testament Church which deals more or less explicitly and extensively with the charismata. For our subject see especially the charisma articles in biblical wordbooks, the commentaries on the charisma texts, the recent study by Georg Eichholz, *Was heisst charismatische Gemeinde?* (Chr. Kaiser Verlag, Munich 1960) and the literature quoted there, especially the dissertation (unpublished) by Friedrich Grau, 'Der neutestamentliche Begriff Charisma' (Tübingen 1946).

relationship between the charismata and the ministry of the laity. This important relationship was seen at Evanston, when in the Section Report on 'The Laity: the Christian in his Vocation', the Assembly stated: 'We must understand anew the implications of the fact that we are all baptized, that, as Christ came to minister, so must all Christians become ministers of his saving purpose *according to the particular gift of the Spirit which each has received.*' The Committee of the Department on the Laity at the Third Assembly of the World Council of Churches at New Delhi reaffirmed this insight when it said that the main concern of the Department is the wish 'to foster a deeper understanding and fuller development of *the varied gifts and ministries of all members of Christ's Body in the world.*' Until now little has been done to elaborate these general statements. The following comments are, therefore, written in the hope that they will foster the study of this vital relationship between the charismata and the ministry of the laity.

I

What are these charismata really? How can they be recognized, and what is their function?

A Pauline Term

When a Roman emperor came to the throne or when he celebrated his birthday, he gave his troops a free gift of money which was called *donativum* or *charisma*. The soldiers had not earned this money as they had earned their pay (*opsōnia*). They received it free, given out of the goodness of the emperor's heart. It was the apostle Paul who began to use this military term for describing God's gracious gifts to man. 'For sin pays an *opsōnia*, and the *opsōnia* is death, but God gives freely, and his *charisma* is eternal life, in union with Christ Jesus our Lord' (Rom. 6.23).

Although the reality designated by the term charismata is a

truth to which other biblical authors also testified, the word itself remained a typical Pauline expression. In Paul's letters the term occurs fourteen times, twice in the Pastoral letters and only once in the rest of the New Testament. Usually one thinks immediately of such specific gifts of grace as mentioned in the lists of charismata of Romans 12.6-8 and I Cor. 12.8-10, 28-30, (and Ephesians 4.11?). But the term means far more than these lists suggest. It is the free gift of God's election, blessing and promises (Rom. 11.29; cf. 9.4-5), of God's grace and forgiveness (Rom. 5.15-16) and of the eternal life (Rom. 6.23). It can describe such special events as God's rescuing in a difficult situation (II Cor. 1.11). Both natural endowments (I Cor. 7.7; I Peter 4.10) and the gift implanted in a man when he is ordained to a special ministry (I Tim. 4.14; II Tim. 1.6) can be called charismata.

Marks of the Charismata and Criteria for discerning them

If the above-mentioned diverse things and events are described as charismata, what are then their constituent elements and marks? How can charismata be discerned?

Paul's terminology in I Cor. 12.4 gives us a clue to the answer. He used there three terms in a complementary way, almost as interchangeable synonyms, namely *charisma*, *diakonia* and *energema*. The term *charisma* designates the source of God's gifts, namely God's mercy and grace. For Paul grace is never general and undifferentiated, but it always takes the form of a concrete 'grace given to me' (Rom. 12.3). In this sense 'everyone has the charisma God has granted him, one this charisma and another that' (I Cor. 7.7). There is a rich diversity of charismata, but all have only one source; the *charis*, God's grace. The term *diakonia* designates the purpose of God's gifts. Each charisma is intimately connected with a vocation (see the connection of these two terms in Rom. 11.29). According to the pattern laid down by Christ, this is always a call to *diakonia*, a call to a special task of service. The term *energema* designates the nature of God's gifts. Each charisma is an energy, an operation of the power of the Holy Spirit. Therefore, Paul called the charismata sometimes *pneumatika*, gifts which manifest the power of the Spirit. Wherever this origin in God's grace, this purpose of service and this truly spiritual energy are manifest, there is charisma.

Another clue to the answer of the above question is Paul's criteria for discerning the charismata. In the introduction to his main chapter on the gifts of the Spirit, Paul wrote: 'No one can say "Jesus is Lord!" except under the influence of the Holy Spirit' (I Cor. 12.3). Without this confession of Christ as the Lord, the charismata cease to be manifestations of the Spirit. Paul had already insisted at the beginning of the same letter that the basic *charis* of God given to the Corinthians is in Christ Jesus and that, therefore, they are not lacking in any charisma (I Cor. 1. 4-7). A charisma can always be recognized where Jesus is allowed to be the Lord. A second criterion for discerning charismata is the statement that 'in each of us the Spirit is manifested in one particular way, for some useful purpose,' in order 'to build up the community' (I Cor. 12.7; 14. 3-5, 26). The charismata are given to us in the first place for our brothers, for the inward and outward growth of the Church. Each charisma is quite personal ('the grace given to me'), yet is never an individualistic gift, but leads to community and integrates into the 'body'. (All charismata lists refer to the Church as a body: Rom. 12.4-5; I Cor. 12.12-27; Eph. 4.12). Finally it is noteworthy that all lists of charismata lead up to the term 'love' (I Cor. 13; Rom. 12.9ff.; Eph. 4.15-16). The charismata have not an aim in themselves, and even the inward and outward building up of the Church is not the ultimate goal. All aim at the harvest of the Spirit which is love, joy, peace ... (Gal. 5.22). Wherever Jesus is allowed to be the Lord, where the Church grows into maturity and fully participates in Christ's mission of love and reconciliation in the world, there is charisma.

The Wrong Equation of the Charismata with Ecstatic Enthusiasm

Usually much emphasis is laid on the extraordinary, enthusiastic or even ecstatic character of the charismata. There are indeed some extraordinary things mentioned such as 'prophecy', 'the speaking in tongues' and 'the working of miracles'. This charismatic enthusiasm is not limited to the Early Church, as many suppose. Wherever the energy of God's grace and Spirit is at work such extraordinary things can happen, even in the midst of an arid Christendom situation (see Johann Christoph Blumhardt's life and work). It is true, however, that this charismatic enthusiasm is typical of first-generation Christians, be it the Christians of the first or second century, new converts in Asia and Africa, or converts from nominal Christianity to Pentecostal churches in Latin America and the West.

The ebbing away of charismatic enthusiasm in the Church of later generations has often been wrongly interpreted as the loss of the Church's charismatic nature. This happened already in the post-apostolic age as can be seen in the writings of Justin, Irenaeus and others who thought that the ecstatic, miraculous element is essential for the charismata and who believed, therefore, that the dwindling of these elements in the Church of their time implied also the disappearance of the charismata. Consequently the traditional Roman Catholic ecclesiology does not mention the charismata, or assumes that they do not belong to the essence of the Church, a statement which nowadays is strongly opposed by Catholic theologians such as Karl Rahner.[1] The same equating of the charismata with an ecstatic

[1] Karl Rahner, 'Das Charismatische in der Kirche', in *Das Dynamische in der Kirche* (Freiburg 1958), pp. 38-73. Based on biblical studies and the statements of the encyclical *Mystici corporis*, this important study by the Austrian Jesuit theologian shows that apart from the charisma of the hierarchy (*Charisma des Amtes*) there are 'non-institutional charismata' which constitute besides the hierarchical structure of the Church a charismatic structure of the Church.

enthusiasm has led many Pentecostalists to write off the 'historic' or 'denominational' churches and to claim that only within the Pentecostal movement are the charismata present in a significant way. It led them to their schematic distinction between regeneration in the conversion experience, water baptism, sanctification and the experience of baptism of the Holy Ghost. It also led them to the questionable singling out of *one* charisma, the speaking in tongues, to become the typical initial manifestation and evidence of baptism by the Holy Spirit and of the receiving of charismata.[1] Again the same equation of the charismata with ecstatic enthusiasm is evident in Max Weber's concept of the 'charismatic lordship'.[2] Although Max Weber borrowed the term charisma from Paul he thoroughly secularized and partly changed it. A confrontation between Paul's and Max Weber's concepts of charisma is most revealing because sometimes Max Weber shows implications which are indeed dormant in Paul's thinking about the charismata, while more often Weber's concept

[1] Harold Horton, *The Gifts of the Spirit* (Assemblies of God Publishing House, London 1954); Earl P. Paulk, *Your Pentecostal Neighbour* (Pathway Press, Cleveland 1958), pp. 61ff., 95ff., 159ff. Today there is a marked change in the relationship between the Pentecostal movement and the 'historic' churches. Two Pentecostal churches were received into the membership of the WCC and the ministry of mutual interpretation done by David J. du Plessis begins to bear fruit; see his brochure: *The Spirit bade me go; the astonishing move of God in the denominational Churches* (Dallas 1961). No serious consideration of the charismata can henceforth escape the Pentecostal challenge 'that no one can ever grasp the full meaning of the charismata until there is an experience similar to that on the day of Pentecost' (du Plessis, *op. cit.*, p. 32). But our Pentecostal brethren will have to face the question of whether it is in accordance with the total biblical teaching about the Spirit, the Church and its ministry to combine in a legalistic way the baptism by the Spirit with charismatic enthusiasm. See the pastoral letter issued by the Dutch Reformed Church in Holland about 'The Church and the Pentecostal Groups', where in a sympathetic way the main concern of the Pentecostal movement is described, critically discussed and partly rejected on the basis of the biblical message ('De Kerk en de Pinkstergroepen', Boekencentrum, s'Gravenhage 1960).

[2] Max Weber, *Wirtschaft und Gesellschaft* (J. C. B. Mohr, Tübingen 1956), pp. 140-48, 555-8, 662-95.

of charisma is so different from Paul's that this very difference accentuates the specific character of Paul's concept.

It is true that often the power of the Spirit shows itself in charismatic enthusiasm. This can be a genuine and healthy manifestation of the charismata and should not be frowned on by 'respectable' churches. Paul wants us to 'be aglow with the Spirit', he admonishes us 'not to quench the Spirit' and he welcomes that we all edify ourselves by speaking enthusiastically in tongues (Rom. 12.11; I Thess. 5.19; I Cor. 14.5). But to equate charismatic manifestations with enthusiastic manifestations is against Paul's teaching. When the Corinthians tended to overestimate charismatic enthusiasm, Paul reminded them that enthusiasm ('being swept off') was a typical part of their heathen past. In his study on 'The Spirit and Enthusiasm', Gottlob Schrenk showed that the terms *enthusiasmos* and *ekstasis* were technical terms in the heathen cults of the early Christians' environment, where the aim was to replace the human *nous* (intelligence and moral judgment) by the Divinity. According to Paul, however, the Spirit uses the *nous*, renewing and guiding it for God's purpose.[1] Paul would, therefore, not agree with Max Weber's opposition between a 'charismatic' and a 'rational' way of leadership. In the Old Testament and in the synoptic gospels, the Spirit was indeed mainly seen in connection with extraordinary manifestations, but Paul considered the fact of whether the Spirit manifests itself in an extraordinary or quite ordinary way as irrelevant. 'The real criterion for measuring the value or lack of value of the gifts of the Spirit is the confession, Jesus is Lord, and at the same time the edification, *oikodome*, the expediency, *sympheron*, of the Church. But this brings us to a completely new understanding of the Spirit.'[2]

[1] Gottlob Schrenk, 'Geist und Enthusiasmus; eine Erläuterung zur paulinischen Theologie', in *Studien zu Paulus* (Zwingli-Verlag, Zürich 1954), pp. 107-124.

[2] Eduard Schweizer, Art. *pneuma*, in Kittel, *Theologisches Wörterbuch zum NT* VI, p. 422, [Engl. *Spirit of God*, p. 67].

This new understanding of the Holy Spirit reveals itself in the charismata lists. They contain many things which are not at all spectacular, but sober gifts which are most precious yet have nothing to do with ecstatic enthusiasm: a word of wisdom, a word of deep knowledge, steadfast fidelity, discernment, teaching, humble service, administration. . . . One could go on, for Paul never claimed to be exhaustive in his lists of charismata. We must have 'the courage for new charismata', as Karl Rahner wrote, which for the most part are what he calls 'small charismata', charismata in everyday life which are seldom noticed by anyone and which are usually not recorded in history because they make no headlines. Paul would surely have been most interested to read what Max Weber wrote many centuries later about the process of charismata becoming part of everyday life (*die Veralltäglichung des Charismatischen*), but he would have described and evaluated this process quite differently from Max Weber.

Charismatic enthusiasm leads to authoritarianism. On the basis of their extraordinary charisma given only to them, enthusiastic charismatics tend to claim an uncritical and blind recognition of their gift and leadership. Max Weber described this convincingly and consequently spoke only about charismatic *lordship* (*charismatische Herrschaft*). But Paul did not identify the charismata with such charismatic enthusiasm. 'Be aglow with the Spirit, *serve the Lord!*' (Rom. 12.11). Unless the charisma leads to *service* (and not lordship), it is no charisma for Paul. Each charismatic must subject himself to the judgment of the congregation which is exhorted: 'Do not quench the Spirit . . . *but test everything*' (I Thess. 5.19-21). Therefore Paul wrote to the Christians in Corinth about the above marks of the true charismata and the criteria of discerning them. The whole point of I Cor. 12-14 is the warning that charismatic enthusiasm should not lord it over the congregation but that each charisma has its appropriate measure, function and time and that all are directed to service. 'Therefore,' comments Karl

Rahner, 'the charisma is always related to suffering. For, to remain in the body, to fulfil the vocation of one's charisma and to endure the counter-pressure of (sometimes equally valid) other charismata is true suffering. Our own gift is always limited and humiliated by the gift of somebody else. Sometimes it has to wait until it can develop itself, until its *kairos* comes when the right time of another has passed or is declining.'[1]

The Supernatural Character of the Charismata

Pentecostal writers insist much on the supernatural character of the charismata—and rightly so. It does not belong to the nature of fallen man to live by grace. The inclinations of his heart tend to self-love rather than service, and his life is under the power of evil forces. Conversion and rebirth must happen before a man can truly acknowledge Christ as the Lord. In this sense charismata are indeed supernatural.

This does not mean that quite natural events and gifts cannot become charismata, i.e. cannot be directed to service, be used by the power of the Spirit and be recognized as a gift of God's free grace. It does mean, however, that we do not possess charismata once and for all. We are their *stewards* and not their owners. They happen to us, become manifest through us, but they are not at our disposal according to our own will, and for our own purposes. While natural gifts, endowments and abilities can become charismata, their character is not in itself charismatic; they can be used by what Paul called 'the flesh' as well as by the Spirit.

The verbs used in connection with the charismata are revealing: Paul hopes to *impart* some spiritual gift to the Church in Rome (Rom. 1.11), and Peter says that we have *received* gifts (I Peter 4.10). From the point of view of God, these gifts are *irrevocable* (Rom. 11.29), but we may *not neglect* them, but must constantly *rekindle* and *earnestly seek* them (I Tim. 4.14; II Tim.

[1] Karl Rahner, *op. cit.*, p. 68f.

195

1.6; I Cor. 12.31). Only in such a way, instantly and *in actu* do we *have* the charismata (Rom. 12.6; I Cor. 7.7).

The Charismata given for serving Church and World

The verbs in the charismata texts reveal also the purpose of these gifts: They are to *strengthen* the local church (Rom. 1.11), so that the Christians can *serve* one another and that the church may be *edified* (I Peter 4.10; I Cor. 14.5). Through such gifts the churches are indeed *enriched* (I Cor. 1.5ff), for the gifts *abound* and bring forth justice, eternal life and thanksgivings (Rom. 5.15f.; 6.23; II Cor. 1.11). The charismata give the ministers in the Church power to practise their total ministry (I Tim. 4.11-16), e.g. to *speak* for the upbuilding, encouragement and consolation of men (Rom. 12.3; I Cor. 14.3). Such ministers are themselves a gift of Christ to the Church, because they are given to foster *the equipment of the saints for the work of ministry* (Eph. 4.7, 11-12).

At first sight the charismata seem to serve only the inward and outward upbuilding of the Church. Are they merely church-directed? In answering this question, A. B. Come's distinction between the primary and diversified church-directed ministries, and the one ultimate world-directed ministry of reconciliation of the Church is helpful: 'Every Christian participates in partial and differing ways in the diversified church-directed ministries for the building up of the Church, the body of Christ, both in quantity of number and in the quality of maturity. Every Christian also participates in the same way as every other Christian in the single world-directed ministry of reconciliation of the world, by allowing God's truth and love revealed in Christ to shine through his life wherever he happens to be and whatever he happens to be doing.' 'The church-directed ministries are first only in order of time because by them an organism (the body of Christ) is built up and maintained and equipped to perform a given task and mission. That mission is ultimate, and it is the clue to the meaning of the Church's very being.'[1] While the charismata are in the first place given for the inward and outward growth of the Church, their ultimate aim, the charismatic 'harvest', is the service of God and the total cosmos.

This break-through of the charismata from a church-centric attitude to service in God's work of love for the world becomes clear in the exegesis of Rom. 12. The charismata are given to the Church for its worship, for its '*Gottesdienst*', its ministry for God. But to Paul this worship was no inner church affair. He claimed the whole world and total life as the temple court of the true spiritual worship in which each member participates with his particular charisma. This worship is celebrated by both those especially noticeable charismata in the church meeting which fulfil representative or leading functions in the Church (verses 6-8) *and* by the charismatic way of life described in the verses 9ff. which mark the life of Christians both in the Christian community (verses 10-13) and in their attitude to all men (12. 14-13. 10). 'It is important to characterize the whole work of the Christian Church as a charismatic work, because in this whole work the spiritual worship in the world is realized.'[2]

The charismata given to Church and world?

Where is the charismatic life described above to be found? Does it characterize only the life of Christians in their corporate life and their life in the world or are charismata given also to persons who do not know the giver of grace? Every honest observer sees that much in the life of the churches and their members is far from charismatic and that much in the life of men and women of other faiths and no faith bears at least some

---

[1] Arnold B. Come, *Agents of Reconciliation* (Westminster Press, Philadelphia 1960), pp. 166, 169.

[2] Ernst Käsemann, 'Gottesdienst im Alltag der Welt (zu Röm. 12)', in *Judentum, Urchristentum, Kirche; Festschrift für Joachim Jeremias* (Töpelmann, Berlin 1960), p. 171. See also Eduard Schweizer, 'Romans 12', *Laity* 12 (October 1961), p. 14.

marks of the charismata. Karl Rahner acknowledges that the charismata are indeed not the exclusive privilege of the Church. 'The grace of Christ embraces man more than we think and it grips the nature of man deeper, more secretly and more comprehensively than we often assume.'[1]

If this is true, can we still speak about 'Church' and 'world' in a static way? Where are the boundaries of the charismatic Church? In his study on 'Body and Body of Christ' Ernst Käsemann showed how the charismata help to strengthen and mature the members of the body to remain in their sacramental being, the Church. This Church 'is the world, in which now everybody has to understand the other as the one who was loved by God in Christ. Where Church and world are put in opposition to one another, there again the appearance and the *sarx* have been made Lord; there even in a supposedly existing Church one is not in Christ who embraces everything as being created and loved by God.' The Church 'becomes worldwide in the *agape*, which understands now all life from the point of view of the charisma given to all life, i.e. from the point of view of all life's membership in the divine creation.'[2]

Paul never wrote in such a way about the charisma of all life. *His* special charisma and ministry concerned the inward and outward growth of local churches, and when he wrote about charismata he spoke about the life and task of baptized believers who know and confess Jesus as the Lord. Yet it is true that because of Paul's teaching about God's all-embracing grace in Christ, his concept of charisma has also a strongly eschatological momentum, aiming at discovering and awakening charismata not only in the Church but in all life unto the ends of the world and the end of time.

[1] Karl Rahner, *op. cit.*, p. 56.
[2] Ernst Käsemann, *Leib und Leib Christi* (J. C. B. Mohr, Tübingen 1933), p. 185.

II

Having attempted to understand and spell out Paul's concept of the charismata, we now turn to discover some of the implications of this concept for the life and work of the charismatic laity.

A People by God's Grace: the Charismatic Status of the Laity

To be the laity, to belong to God's people, cannot make us proud. It is not by our merit that we are called to be members of Christ's body and fellow workers of God, but wholly by grace. This charismatic status of the laity fills us with wonder and not with pride. Wherever Christians begin to look down on men of other faiths or no faith they lose their charismatic status and herewith their true church membership.

We are not born into this charismatic status. Du Plessis was right when in his emphatic Pentecostal way he stated that 'God has no grandsons.'[1] To become the laity each one must indeed be born anew, converted or, as Paul usually put it, crucified and buried with Christ and thus transformed into his likeness, transferred from the realm of the 'flesh' into the realm of the Spirit, from the present age into the age to come and from the old world with its powers and principalities into the New Creation. 'You are now the people of God, who once were not his people; outside his mercy once, you have now received mercy', you have now experienced God's grace and received your charismatic status (I Peter 2.10).

It is no wonder that this key text for the correct understanding of the ministry of the laity occurs in a letter which in its substance was originally probably an exhortation to people who had just been baptized. The charismatic status of the laity is intimately connected with baptism. This is most clearly expressed in the Orthodox baptismal liturgy which—like baptism in the Ancient Church—includes the renunciation of

[1] D. J. du Plessis, *op. cit.*, pp. 63-70.

the Devil, the act of baptism, and the act of chrismation. If the act of renunciation seals the process of conversion and the act of baptism gives the assurance of the forgiveness of sins, the act of chrismation initiates the 'people by God's grace' into its charismatic status. Every word and act in this office of chrismation is significant:

> The priest anoints with the holy Chrism the person who has been baptized, making the sign of the cross: on the brow, on the eyes, the nostrils, the lips, the ears, the breast, and on the hands and feet, saying each time, 'The seal of the gift of the Holy Spirit. Amen.' Then the priest, accompanied by the sponsors and the baptized, makes the circuit of the font three times, and all sing, 'As many as have been baptized into Christ have put on Christ. Alleluia.' Two lessons from Holy Scripture are then read; first, Romans 6.3-11, and then, Matt. 28.16-20. Read at this point of the service, both lessons have their specific significance. The passage from the Epistle to the Romans points to the life in the power of the Holy Spirit to which the newly baptized has been called. The lesson from Matthew recalls Christ's commandment to teach and baptize all nations. Both texts confirm the commitment of the newly baptized. The service ends with a prayer of intercession.[1]

This liturgy shows the truth of what the Orthodox theologian Leo Zander said: 'The Church is, therefore, not only the body of Christ and the community of the saints, but also the continuous Pentecost, the personal relation of all believers with all three persons of the Holy Trinity.'[2]

Where this continuous Pentecost, this charismatic status of the laity, does not manifest itself, something is wrong with the Church and its members. We need not agree with the Pentecostal definition of the initial manifestation of the Spirit, but

[1] Lukas Vischer, *Ye are Baptised;* a study of Baptism and Confirmation liturgies as the Initiation to the Ministry of the Laity (published by the Department of the Laity, WCC, Geneva 1961), p. 18.
[2] Leo Zander, 'Die orthodoxe Kirche', in *Und ihr Netz zerriss* (Quell-Verlag, Stuttgart 1957), p. 131. See also Nikos A. Nissiotis, 'Le sacerdoce charismatique, le laïcat et l'autorité pastorale', *Verbum Caro* 55 (Neuchâtel 1960), pp. 217-38.

the Pentecostal reminder that our charismatic status must become manifest is quite pertinent and true. This challenge must not lead us to the Pentecostal separation of the baptism by water and by the Spirit, but it must steep us in a deeper participation in the liturgical and sacramental life of the Church and a deeper study of the biblical message: We can indeed 'be severed from Christ' and 'fall out of grace' (Gal. 5.4). Our charismatic status is indeed not in our possession. It must be continually nurtured and upheld through a steadfast devotion 'to the apostles' teaching and brotherly fellowship, to the breaking of the bread and the prayers' (Acts 2.42).

The charismatic status gained and maintained in the way described here opens the 'people by God's grace' for the world. In the course of the history of salvation God's grace seemed for a long time limited to the chosen people Israel. Yet even then Abraham was blessed in order 'that all the families on earth shall be blessed' (Gen. 12.3). Even then the waters of God's grace were not wholly held back by the walls of Israel's Temple; a small stream flowed out from below the threshold of the Temple to become the river of life-giving water in the world (Ezek. 47.1-10). But at Pentecost, the dams of the lake of grace burst and God's grace is now flooding the world. God's people is now being gathered out of the heathen nations, a revolutionary fact which even such a self-conscious Israelite as James had to admit (Acts 15.14)! This flood of grace penetrating the world and its history constantly upsets the border line between Church and world. Our charismatic status constantly forces us to go beyond the Church boundaries and to be a witness to God's world-embracing grace.

Attaining Mature Manhood: the Charismatic Growth of the Laity

It is not enough to preserve the charismatic status. The charismata give not only the steadfast knowledge that we are anchored in God's grace, but they are also the channel for the energy of the Holy Spirit. The charismata continually upset our thinking and acting, because they lead us to acknowledge Christ as Lord and not ourselves, our idols or the idols of our time. This revolutionary and renewing power becomes active in our lives and lets us grow into maturity. What are the marks of this charismatic maturity which we are called to attain?

Through Christ's definitive sacrifice at the cross, God's people needs no more the mediation of human priests. The spiritual immaturity of Old Testament times has now come to an end. Since Pentecost the Spirit is no more limited to priests, prophets and kings, but all who have received the charismatic status are now 'a royal priesthood' which can prophesy, because all have received the Spirit. All are now *theodidaktoi*, i.e. people who are being taught by God himself in the wisdom of love (I Thess. 4.9). As the mature laity we are, therefore, freed from legalism, from the tyranny of the 'musts' and 'must nots'. No more conforming to such criteria of the present age. Continually being transformed by the renewal of our minds (our *nous*), we must now be able to discern by ourselves the will of God (Rom. 12.2). This will of God is always concrete, just as the grace of God is. Each charisma contains a specific *klesis*, a vocation. It belongs to our charismatic maturity to discern and accept in each new given time and place the concrete vocation and task given to us by God. This frees us from the curse of having constantly to compare ourselves with others. There is no longer a place for superiority complexes: 'Do not be conceited or think too highly of yourself' (Rom. 12.3). In view of the Roman situation it was probably not necessary for Paul to add: 'Do not have inferiority complexes or think too lowly of yourself', but such an apostolic exhortation would be healthy for many laymen and lay women today, because inferiority complexes (especially 'Christian' ones) are a sign of immaturity. Another mark of maturity is to be sensitive to new charismata and vocations given to us and our brothers. Because of their supernatural character, charismata are always astonishing, shocking and sometimes frightening.

They tend to disturb established patterns. In maturity we must dare to expect and pray for such new charismata, to discover and examine them and accordingly either to give them free course or discipline them. Finally, the growth into charismatic maturity is a growth into spontaneity. The charismatic laity need not be mobilized for this or that church activity, because its whole life has a worship, witness and service dimension, its whole life radiates grace and ripens the harvest of the Spirit.

Charismatic maturity does not mean, however, that we can now do without the Christian community. On the contrary, the charismata insert us into the body of Christ and herewith into a concrete local church. This Christian community on all its levels from the house-church to the world-wide Christian fellowship is the God-given place of growth into maturity. In this community our brothers and sisters (who are some-times quite tiresome) are given to us; we cannot choose them according to our own liking. Here we are to learn patience, mutual submission, forgiveness and love. Here we are trained to accept our limitation, to wait for the right time (the *kairos*) and to use our gifts of grace for the common good, for the upbuilding of the Church. In an examination of the biblical terms 'orderliness', 'order' and 'maturity', P. A. van Stempvoort has shown the intimate connection between the ordering of the diverse charismata and the growth in maturity. Without this ordering the charismata would lead to destructive chaos.[1] But we must immediately add that 'order' (*taxis*) in the New Testament never means a predetermined, static order of a fixed pattern, structure or system, but it is the strategic battle-order of the *militia Christi* in which the different units (*taxeis*) of charismata must fight in good order (*kata taxin*). This order must, therefore, constantly be adapted to the new charismata given within a concrete Christian community and according to each new challenge which is to be met by the ministry of

[1] P. A. van Stempvoort, *Decorum, Orde en Mondigheid in het Nieuew Testament* (Callenbach N.V., Nÿkerk 1956).

God's people.[1] The aim of the ordering of the charismata is not the strait-jacket of the Prussian *'Ordnung muss sein!'* but the *peace* of God (I Cor. 14.33).

Such growth into charismatic maturity by our membership in the corporate life of God's people could deteriorate into an inward looking churchism, where the insistence on the edification of one another becomes an excuse for forgetting 'the others' outside the church walls. This development can be observed in certain 'lay movements', but it is the opposite of the calling of a true lay movement. The maturity of the 'royal priesthood' is exactly its openness to the world, its priestly ministry of representing the world before God and representing God to the world, accomplished in costly service.

Elected for Service: the Charismatic Ministry of the Laity

The charismata mould us into the form of the servant. The charismatic status leads to the charismatic ministry. This ministry must be fulfilled according to the pattern laid down by *the* Minister, Christ: the mature laity is 'permitted and enabled to share in the continuing high-priestly work of Christ by offering themselves in love and obedience to God and in love and service of men.'[2]

Everything said so far is true for all members of God's people, for 'ordinary' Christians as well as for bishops, theologians and ordained ministers. All share in this costly charismatic ministry. Therefore all need to receive the charismatic status and all must attain charismatic maturity. In a living church every member has, therefore, something to contribute to the inward and outward growth of the Christian community. Each of the manifold charismata and ministries is indispensable and important for the right functioning of the body (I Cor.

[1] P. A. van Stempvoort, *Eenheid en Schisma* (Callenbach N.V., Nÿkerk 1950), pp. 94ff.

[2] T. W. Manson, *Ministry and Priesthood: Christ's and Ours* (Epworth Press, London 1958) p. 70.

12.12–27). While most churches pay lip service to this fundamental biblical truth, only a few actually encourage the
development of the charismata and ministries of all. Not many
church constitutions include paragraphs such as the following,
taken from the chapter on 'The Ministry of the Laity' in the
Constitution of the Church of South India:

> The Church 'welcomes and will as far as possible provide for the
> exercise by lay persons, both men and women, of such gifts of
> prophecy, evangelization, teaching, healing and administration
> as God bestows upon them.' The Church 'desires that all its
> members should constantly bear in mind that their different forms
> of ministry both to those within the Church and to those outside
> it, are only of value for the carrying out of God's purposes in so
> far as the Divine Spirit is working through those ministries on the
> hearts of men. The ministry of intercession, therefore, is vital, and
> it should not only underlie and inspire all those other ministries
> that are detailed in this chapter, but be recognised as one which
> should constantly be exercised by all members of the Church.[1]

The same Constitution states, however, clearly that within
this ministering people and for the sake of it some special
ministries are given to the Church. Certain charismata such as
the gifts of Christian teaching, oversight and assistance in the
congregation must indeed become public because of the very
nature of the ministry involved. They are, therefore, recognized
and set apart by the Church for this purpose. This is one of the
main origins of the specially ordained and set-apart ministry
in the Church.[2] These set-apart ministers have in accordance

---

[1] *The Constitution of the Church of South India* (C.L.S., Madras 1952), pp.
34, 37.
[2] It is impossible to elaborate a full doctrine of the set-apart ministry
merely on the basis of the New Testament message about the charismata,
just as it is impossible to base the ecclesiology exclusively on the charismata
passages. For a fuller treatment of this question see 'Ministers of the priestly
people', *Laity* 9 (July 1960), pp. 5–21 and the literature referred to in that
article. See also the too schematic but helpful distinction between two
complementary aspects or structures in the Church, namely the 'institution'
and the 'event' (or charisma) in J. L. Leuba, *L'Institution et l'Evénement*
(Delachaux et Niestlé, Neuchâtel 1950) and K. Rahner, *op. cit.*

with their particular charismata to serve the Church, to call it constantly to its charismatic status and to assist it in its charismatic growth. They do so by giving thanks to God for his manifold grace manifesting itself in the charismatic Church, by teaching about this grace of God (being preachers of the Gospel rather than of legalism!) by administering the sacraments of grace, by exhorting on the basis of this grace, and by interceding for God's congregation that it may grow in grace. This will open their eyes to the charismata given to each member of God's people and it will enable them to harmonize these gifts, to let them develop and direct them to service.

However, by no means all charismata are in this way made public and set apart for service mainly within and to God's people. The greatest part of the Church's charismatic energy is used for the ministry of reconciliation in and for the world. 'God has designed the Church in his calling so that the large bulk of its membership does not, cannot, live withdrawn within the sanctuary of the Church but is buried like seed, like leaven, like salt, like light, in the earth of common humanity. Through them, he is working his will for mankind, bringing the world to crisis and ultimately to reconciliation.'[1]

[1] Arnold B. Come, *op. cit.*, p. 170.

YOUTH AND THE ECUMENICAL MOVEMENT

Philip Potter

W. A. VISSER 'T HOOFT has for the past forty years been identified with the Ecumenical Movement, and particularly with the place of youth in it. With him the role of youth in the life of the Church moved from being a pious exhortation to a dynamic reality. He gave the greatest impetus in this century to youth being at the forefront of the battle of the Church militant rather than trailing behind waiting to take the place of weary, battered warriors. This achievement was one which began with himself and it was based on his overwhelming sense of the sufficiency of God. Because God alone in Christ is sufficient to do his work among men, those who have accepted him gladly by faith, be they young or old, are given an astonishing freedom from the coils of immobile tradition, complacency and fear. They are accorded the glad fearlessness of bearing to be the instruments of the liberating, directing and creative Spirit, as fellow-workers with God in his world and among his people.

When I first met and heard Visser 't Hooft at the Oslo World Conference of Christian Youth in 1947, he was nearly 47. Yet the fire was still burning in his belly, and it was he more than any other speaker who set the hearts of so many of us burning in utter reliance on the sufficiency of God, not as a means of having a haven of spiritual security in a troubled world, but as the driving force to total self-commitment to the Lord's business. 'Youth,' he said to us, 'has a specific task, a definite contribution and the right to accomplish that task and to make that contribution. . . . We are here to proclaim the great astounding fact: that he is the Lord. . . . The Church is militant, and only militant, if it lives wholly out of this unshakable certainty. . . . The Church is not condemned to remain static, sleepy, unfaithful and unimaginative. For he liberates it from its self-made prison and works its rebirth. Youth need not despair, for he calls it into his service and gives it a revolutionary and world-embracing task to accomplish.'

Since Oslo the resolve to devote my energies, along with others, to the renewal of the life of the churches that they may be ready for mission in the world and may grow into manifest unity, has happily led me to be his colleague in the World Council of Churches and to continue to draw inspiration from his amazingly youthful and pungent mind. What follows is an attempt to restate, with the inevitable help of Dr Visser 't Hooft's writings, the place of youth in the Ecumenical Movement as it has developed, and now that the World Council of Churches has become a large, highly organized and articulate body.

'It is the fever of youth which keeps the world at its normal temperature. When youth becomes cold the teeth of the rest of the world begin to chatter. . . . I believe that the modern world sins against the spirit of youth, and that this crime will mean the death of that world.' These powerful words of Georges Bernanos were quoted in 1938 by Visser 't Hooft in an article entitled 'What Youth is Seeking—What Youth is Finding'. His own comment was: 'Youth becomes cold when it follows idols. It needs the experience of the disciples on the road to Emmaus who said to each other after the Stranger had left them: "Did not our hearts burn within us while he talked to us on the road, while he opened to us the Scriptures?"'

When Visser 't Hooft came on the world scene in 1924 as
secretary for youth work in the World Alliance of YMCAs,
youth participated in the reigning conceptions of the time—
personal freedom and self-expression (cf. Aldous Huxley's
Do What You Will), autonomy, the rights of the individual.
Youth movements in Europe and elsewhere were concerned to
exploit this philosophy of autonomous living, with the ground
bass of *laissez-faire* liberalism still beating on the air. In the
churches, too, youth movements were separate from the main
stream of church life. Young people were pumped with a
liberal view of Jesus as hero and friend, and were encouraged
to go on a great adventure of personal fulfilment. But they
did not count much in the life of their churches. Churchmen
were content to say, 'Youth are the church of tomorrow.'
Moreover, churches were generally complacent about their
divisions. They shared the reigning conceptions of individualism, competition and live and let live. Then came the crash of
the Depression and the rapid spread of totalitarian mass movements—Communist, Fascist and Socialist. These quickly
mobilized a spiritually unemployed and atomized generation of
young people and made them the spearhead of their vigorous
collectivist, nationalist, and revolutionary movements. The
mass movements had three purposes: to sweep away a decadent
society which was based on empty idealism, community-
destroying individualism, and purposeless pursuit of self-
expression; to rally people behind dominating ideas such as
nationalism and world communism; and to create a sense of
solidarity and obedience to authority in the pursuit of common
goals. Young people quickly supported such movements.

Visser 't Hooft, writing at the time, explains why they did:
'Youth's realism consists in the fact that they do not consider
their life as an end in itself, that they seek for a purpose and
meaning beyond themselves, and that they have discovered
that only such a cause or message is worthy of an unreserved

and total loyalty which carries its authority within itself and which has the quality of absoluteness and dares to claim obedience. They are realistic in the sense that they reject ideals which are mere ideals, ideology which is mere ideology, and that they reverence convictions which express themselves in lives of power. . . . To them life consists not of intellectual, cold-blooded reasoning, but of choice and commitment. . . . In this way the whole life of youth is gradually taking on a character of great simplicity, almost of primitiveness. . . . Life has become much more like a study in black and white. It asks radical questions and demands radical answers. . . . There are choices to be faced and commitments to be made and afterwards causes to be served and commandments to be obeyed. It would seem that the world is entering upon a time of decisions and youth gets ready to play its part in this setting.'

It was in the midst of this struggle that Visser 't Hooft, from the vantage point of the World Student Christian Federation, brought together two central realities which had a powerful effect on Christian youth and students and gave a new direction to the then still young ecumenical movement. He enunciated the totalitarian nature of the Christian Faith and the absolute necessity of the Christian community in an increasingly totalitarian, collectivist and divided world: '*Now* is the time for *radical* Christianity. . . . There is a message of God to us in this new situation. It is that in our proclamation by word and deed we should be much more direct, depend less on outward attractions, outward apologies, outward support of the message, that we should be more single-hearted in our devotion and more radical in our obedience. . . . The main job of the Christian community and the greatest service which it can render to the world is—to *be* the Christian community . . . It must mobilize and awaken the dormant forces of Christian community and demonstrate in its own life that these are actually stronger than the barriers which separate nation from nation, class from class, race from race. And it must challenge its members, not merely to be good individual Christians but to be conscious members of the one world-wide Body which is not identical with any particular church organization, but which is to be reflected by the empirical churches. Such conscious membership implies a sense of solidarity, a willingness to suffer together, a determination not to let oneself be cut off from fellow Christians by any event, not even by war or revolution, and a burning desire to realize the visible unity of the Church.'

These statements were made before the Oxford Conference of 1937 and before Visser 't Hooft became general secretary of the Committee which would set up the World Council of Churches. But they constitute the two foci of his great contribution to the ecumenical movement and especially to Christian youth. Ever since the first World Conference of Christian Youth in Amsterdam in 1939, when he again repeated his main themes, two generations of Christian youth have become more committed to the total claims of Christ and therefore to active critical participation in the life of the churches set as they are to be in the world for its redemption. It is this totality of the claims of Christ on his Body, the Church and on its members, which lies behind the role of youth in the ecumenical movement. Youth in effect took up the challenge he expressed so vigorously in his book, *None other Gods*, which summarized his thinking and writing over the 1920s and 1930s, and which preceded by only one year his appointment as General Secretary of the World Council of Churches in process of formation:

> Our first task is to enter into this Church, and so to demonstrate that we want to be concrete Christians and not merely idea-Christians; but our second task is to fight for the Church against the churches, to protest in the name of the Christian Community against the caricatures of the Christian Community. If we protested from some secure place outside the Church, we should become Pharisees; but if we enter into its ranks, live and toil with

it, and then protest against ourselves as well as against others, we may help to build the true Church, which will certainly be far from perfect, but which may at least be conscious of its own particular mission (pp. 74-5).

Does Visser 't Hooft's message for youth hold good for today, twenty-five years after he gave full expression to it in word and action? Certainly the world of the 1960s is very different from that of the 1920s and 1930s. The Second World War and the subsequent cold war shattered whole-hearted reliance on ideologies, collectivisms and powerful personalities. Young people, living in the ideological camps of both East and West, are not easily taken in by the messianisms of the secular prophets. They detest the hysterical efforts at creating a yawning gulf between peoples by the device of hurling slogans at each other and easy accusing generalizations about each other. They have lost confidence in the idealisms of their elders who were powerless to avert disaster and who have left them to pick up the spiritual débris. They distrust all talk of building a better world, all utopias and blue-prints. They are very down-to-earth and concrete, concerned about what is to be done now. They are capable, on occasion, as in Cuba, Korea and Turkey, of helping to overthrow a government. They will fight a clear issue, such as racial discrimination in the U.S.A. They will take the admitted madness of nuclear warfare seriously enough to demonstrate against it in the Campaign for Nuclear Disarmament and face imprisonment, if need be. They will, when given the chance, insist on hearing the other side of the ideological debate. They refuse to fight the old battles of their elders, as in Socialist parties in the West. In so far as they are involved in the selfish pursuit of their own well-being in the welfare states of the West, or the socialist states of the East, or the emerging states of Asia, Africa and Latin America, they are no worse than their elders who all too often lecture them in public while encouraging them in private. This very fact intensifies their hardly disguised contempt for the older generation.

This new posture of youth in the Western countries (including Russia and the Eastern European states) has been focussed even more sharply in the post-war appearance of the Teenager as a distinct age group in modern society. This age-group (14-19) has adopted its own means of expression in dress, music, the coffee bar, etc. It has compelled governments to rethink its education and its place in society. It has forced commerce to give attention to its needs. The teenagers have surprised the older generation, who postponed their adulthood to the age of 21, by showing much maturity in their thinking and attitudes, while their emotional immaturity is no greater than a 'mixed-up' society which is finding it difficult to keep pace spiritually with its own material progress.

Another radical change is the rapid emergence of the countries of Asia and Africa as independent states in the world community. Visser 't Hooft wrote in the '20s and '30s mainly about the youth of the West, and particularly about European youth. He was, of course, quite aware of the nationalist movements in Asia and applied his own thinking very helpfully to the debates of Christian students in India and Indonesia. But since 1938 these continents have come into their own. The students of the '20s and '30s became the *avant-garde* of liberation movements from colonialist rule. Today, Asia, Africa and Latin America account for some two-thirds of the world's population, and nearly 51 per cent of their population is under 20 years of age. They are all undergoing political and social revolutions, and young people are right in the centre of these 'revolutions of rising expectations'.

The special feature of the Asian and African scene is the violent clash of traditional, indigenous cultures and Western technological civilization. The old is being challenged and even swept away, while the new has displayed very definite defects especially in two world wars, the nuclear menace and the grasping self-assertiveness of its progeny—industrial materialism, whether capitalist or communist. The dilemma created in the soul of the young Asian and African is best expressed by a Nigerian girl:

> Here we stand
> infants overblown,
> poised between two civilizations,
> finding the balance irksome,
> itching for something to happen
> to tip us one way or the other,
> groping in the dark for a helping hand—
> and finding none.
> I'm tired. O my God, I'm tired,
> I'm tired of hanging in the middle way—
> But where can I go?[1]

Behind this cry for direction is a longing for a way of life and a community which can be the soil of natural spiritual growth and well-being. Hence the search in Africa for the 'African personality' or *négritude*, and the great struggle in Asia to build the new society on the renovated foundations of ancient culture and religion.

Underlying all these changes is the accelerated dominance of scientific and technological thinking, no longer as a Western phenomenon, but as a universally accepted world-view. Science has successfully isolated various aspects of nature and of human life and institutions, and extended our mastery of them through patient study, experimentation, verification, and fearless application. This habit of not resting at a particular body of knowledge, but always testing, experimenting and pressing beyond the frontiers of the known and accepted, has infected all domains of human thinking, not least biblical studies. Progress has also come through a widening community of scientists and scholars who can test each other's thought and experiments. Moreover, the application of new insights into nature's working has provided the means of improving the lot of man and of achieving a fuller and richer life, as well as of

[1] Mabel Imoukhude Jolaoso, 'Conflict', published in the magazine *Odù*, Nigeria 1956.

destroying himself. It has certainly brought home to man the necessity of choice, of experimenting, of mastering his world. There is nothing static about such an attitude of mind. Everything is open and big with possibilities. As more and more young people around the world are introduced to the processes of secondary and university education, they imbibe this enquiring and venturing spirit. They are not concerned so much with the fact that something has existed or exists, or to ask what it is, but how it functions, and how it can best function to meet the needs of man now.

The cumulative effect of these changes in the mood of youth throughout the world has created a new situation for the Church. This is all the more evident as our world has become, in many ways, one, through easier communications and the mass media. Happily Visser 't Hooft's emphasis on a vital Christian message and community has found expression in the rapid growth of the ecumenical movement with its twin accent on biblical renewal and the renewal of the churches for mission to the world and for manifest unity. And in this movement he has played no small part through his writings, addresses, travels around the world, and his own work in the World Council of Churches. Young people have therefore found it easier to accept the challenge that Visser 't Hooft sounded in the '30s now than they could have done then.

The biblical renewal has disclosed for young people the dynamic nature of the Christian faith. God is known by his acts. The biblical record is one of God leading his pilgrim people on to repentance and renewal of life and witness. God's decisive interventions in history were very concrete and particular—a people, Israel, and a person, Christ. Through the Holy Spirit God has promised new things to happen in his world through his people, and has given the freedom to perform them. Faith is essentially a commitment, an adventure, an experiment, beginning with Abraham and continuing in union with the ascended Christ. Moreover, the modern discoveries of psychology and the social sciences have enabled us to appreciate more fully the realism of the biblical understanding of man and society, their nature, their quirks and their destiny. This vivid presentation of the Word of God has had a profound effect on young people. It has spoken to them in ways which they understand and on which they can take their stand.

The re-discovery of the nature and mission of the Church has been heartily welcomed by the young people. The Church as the Pilgrim People of God called to leave behind the dead past and march on by faith to declare the wonderful works of God in Christ; the Church as the Body of Christ who forsook the safe haven of Judaism and set his face steadfastly towards Jerusalem to face the death of the Cross and be raised to life for the life of the world; the Church as the servant of the Lord who did not consider his function as being one of lording it over the world but as being its servant even unto death; the Church as the communion of the saints called to be filled with the life of God and to be sent into the world to fill it with the life of God; the Church as the community of pardoned sinners who share the sinful life of the world but offer to the Redeemer a real sacrifice of penitence and intercession for the world; the Church as the communion of all of whatever race or nation or class or sex or age who are being knit together into a new humanity. All these biblical portrayals of the Church have an immediate appeal for young people. Visser 't Hooft's call to young people to enter the ranks of the Church and live and toil with it, has certainly been heeded.

Indeed, since the formation of the WCC, young people have played a not inconspicuous role in its counsels. It was Visser 't Hooft himself who took the initiative in setting up a Youth Department. Thousands of youth and students have participated in the work of the WCC, as well as in the traditional youth ecumenical movements of the YMCA, YWCA and the WSCF. Through ecumenical conferences, consultations, work camps and service projects they have brought something of their realistic, energetic thinking and action to bear on the Church's life and witness in and for the world.

Youth's predilection for the concrete and the manageable has been demonstrated in the ready response of Christian youth to work among refugees, or to offer to give some period of their lives in service wherever it is required at home and abroad. The attitude of mind which sees our world as capable of scientific and technological transformation for the benefit of man disposes them to attack what they consider to be the immobile institutions of introverted churches, and to challenge them to more flexible and mobile structures for meeting the needs of men as the Pilgrim People of God. The fact of our one world makes them impatient of ancient racial and nationalist feuds, and eager to enter into new forms of brotherhood through participation in the Church which has no frontiers of race or nation. Their agony in living in the midst of clashing cultures and of thought forms and confessional formulae which do not speak to men today, drives them to find new ways of confessing their faith and of expressing it in art, drama and life.

Young people have found that this dynamic life and witness together across confessions and denominations has been tolerated and even encouraged on a world, regional or national scale, but very much frowned on locally. They find their church leaders adopting a very schizophrenic attitude to the Ecumenical Movement—ecumenical 'abroad' and denominational 'at home' and keeping the two apart from each other. Young Christians discover in ecumenical discussions and documents much that the churches are willing to agree upon; but they notice, too, an equal unwillingness to put these agreements to the test in acts of obedience for fear of what might happen to hallowed denominational traditions and institutions. They observe a general tendency on the part of churches, singly or together, to lecture the world on issues of war and peace, racial tension and aid to underdeveloped countries, but to be little disposed to make a bold witness through the courageous action of the Christian Community as citizens.

Christian young people are not spectators of these attitudes and actions, nor are they just armchair critics. They are active members of their churches, and it is as such that they are selected and sent to participate in ecumenical activities. But when they have caught a vision of the Church as it ought to be and as it is unfolded in ecumenical thinking, they are moved to make new ventures of faith with their elders in the company of the faithful.

The real danger of the ecumenical movement is precisely this inertia of the denominations and confessions and of churches in a given locality. Indeed, at New Delhi, the World Council of Churches Assembly affirmed that the unity for which the churches must pray and work is that of 'all in each place . . . holding one apostolic faith . . . and having a corporate life reaching out in witness and service to all . . .' The word 'place' was defined as the 'local neighbourhood and also, under modern conditions, of other areas in which Christians need to express unity in Christ', including school, factory, office and congregation. It is here that youth can play a vital role in the ecumenical movement today. The WCC is now so big and well organized and secure in the care of the ecclesiastical pundits and theological wizards that youth's role there will mainly be one of apprenticeship and occasional prodding, highly important though this is. Perhaps the world youth movements of the YMCA, YWCA and the WSCF, because of their greater freedom, can still pioneer in thinking and action as they did in earlier decades, remembering that Visser 't Hooft himself was both a product and leader of two of these movements. But the real battles for the renewal of the churches and for the soul of the ecumenical movement have to be fought 'in each place', within and through the churches.

Visser 't Hooft has, with his customary prescience, stated this clearly and powerfully to the Ecumenical Youth Assembly in Europe 1960:

> We must recapture the faith and vision that lies at the heart of the Ecumenical Movement and that not only for ourselves but for our local congregations. . . . At this point youth in the Ecumenical Movement has a special mission, the mission of refusing to be content with the ecumenical *status quo*, and of keeping up all the pressure they can on their churches. But it must be remembered that the key to the situation is in the local congregation. As long as we have self-centred, isolated local churches we must not expect to advance toward a Church living in fellowship and rendering a united witness to the world. We must, therefore, accept to fight the ecumenical battle where that battle is hardest, that is, in the ordinary life of the ordinary congregation.

The young people at Lausanne responded with alacrity to Visser 't Hooft's challenge by asserting:

> We are agreed that we are more than ever committed to our local churches. But we belong to them now as people who know that in our local church the whole Church is supposed to be there for the whole world in its need. We belong to our local churches henceforth as restless and impatient members called to critical participation . . . We are going home as Christians who know ourselves to have been made responsible by God for seeing that in our own denominations uneasiness about disunity and the passionate longing for visible unity grow constantly. . . .
> We go home to our local churches with the question as to how far these local churches are willing to fulfil, and capable of fulfilling, the mission of Jesus Christ, as to how far we ourselves are willing and capable. . . .
> We go home with the urgent question as to whether the mission of the local church is not best fulfilled by small, flexible, closely-knit communities of people living or working together, communities which by their presence in the everyday world of today, by the manner of their life together, and by the fact of their being unconditionally at the disposal of their fellow men, create trust and bear witness to the reality of Christ's presence.

THE SUFFICIENCY OF GOD

Charles C. West

A T the conclusion of the first assembly of the World
Council of Churches at Amsterdam two architects of
the ecumenical movement, Dr D. T. Niles of Ceylon
and Dr Visser 't Hooft, were discussing what had happened.
'What are your thoughts on the future of this Council,' asked
Niles, 'when the first enthusiasm of the churches coming
together here has worn off?'

'It is most important', replied Visser 't Hooft after a moment's
reflection, 'that we do not decide that we *shall* succeed.'

Since that time the World Council of Churches has become
a highly successful organization. It has gained an ecclesiastical
significance which no church however large and powerful
can any longer ignore. Its intellectual leadership has been
reflected in the theology of every corner of Christendom. Its
political and social influence has reached far beyond the
constituency of its members, into such disparate situations as the
refugee needs of Hong Kong and the racial tensions of South
Africa. Whether agreeable to them or not, the World Council
has become a force in the modern world with which other
centres of power and influence, both religious and secular,
must reckon.

With this success have come both a calling, and a host of
problems. The calling is clearly to broaden the base of

ecumenical work. An ever-wider variety of churches, from Pentecostal to Orthodox, must be included in the policy-making and staff work of the World Council of Churches. More points of view must be brought into dialogue and community if not into agreement with one another. At the same time the increasing complexity of world problems demands a more specialized approach through experts in a number of fields. Gone are the days when a few pioneers of genius and insight could range over the field of faith and order, and life and work, giving prophetic and ecclesiastical leadership to the whole Christian world. Their place is being taken by the patient organization of study and service, the building of a new kind of authority, no less charismatic perhaps but less personalized, more schooled in the art of diplomacy and the science of expert knowledge.

The problems flow from this very structure which success and its consequences require. No longer is the ecumenical movement only a community of adventurous minds and spirits who have found one another across the boundaries of their separated cultures and confessions. It is a representative organization of member churches. No longer are major ecumenical conferences and assemblies events at which new words of prophecy and new discoveries of Christian truth are expected to illuminate the churches, but rather meetings in which the day to day work of study, mission and service is collated and certified by church representatives. Because of its very effectiveness, the ecumenical movement has become wedded to ecumenical institutions. Organization has interposed itself between the work of the Spirit and the works of Christians, as both a channel, and an obstruction.

The result is that the World Council of Churches has aroused all the reactions which every effective force in modern society evokes. It has disappointed idealists who hoped for a pure kingdom of the Spirit, and it has tempted schemers in both church and world to intrigue within it for their own ends. It has been praised as the meeting place of the whole diverse variety of non-Roman Christendom, and blamed for the executive diplomacy by which this coterie is kept from irrelevant controversy and brought to focus on the central issues. It has been chided for the lack of prophetic originality in the reports of its assemblies, and resented when it takes action or speaks sharply to an issue which violates the sensibility of a minority. It is called on to deal authoritatively with the whole range of problems which concern the mission, unity and service of the Church and warned that even its overworked, undermanned staff is in danger of falling victim to Parkinson's Law, and of imposing a new bureaucracy on Christendom.

All of these are real problems, not only of the World Council of Churches, but of any powerful organization in the modern world. They are insoluble problems, on each of which no more than an uneasy compromise can be reached, which is forever in danger of breaking down. There is no idealism whereby a church organization on any level can avoid the question to its institutional existence which they pose: is this organization useful enough, dynamic and effective enough in pursuing its proper ends, to be worth the risk which its influence and self-assertion entails? Is it enough of a servant of the purpose of God to overbalance its tendency to become an end in itself? The answer, whether for a local congregation, a denominational headquarters, a bishop's office, or the World Council of Churches, will always be only a qualified yes, challenged by a no which demands repentance and reform.

Ecumenical Ministry: Paul

The writers who have composed this book are as aware of this problem as the man whom it honours. Echoes of it are found in almost every chapter. What, then, in the midst of the dilemmas of worldly success, is the ministry laid on the World Council of Churches by its Lord? It is this question which brings us to a closer look at the Pauline passage from which the title of this book was taken and which each contributor had in mind when he wrote.

> Are we beginning to commend ourselves again? Or do we need, as some do, letters of recommendation to you, or from you? You yourselves are our letter of recommendation, written on your hearts to be known and read by all men; and you show that you are a letter from Christ delivered (ministered) by us, written not with ink but with the Spirit of the living God, not on tablets of stone but on tablets of human hearts.
>
> Such is the confidence that we have through Christ toward God. Not that we are sufficient of ourselves to claim anything as coming from us; our sufficiency is from God, who has qualified us to be ministers of a new covenant, not in a written code but in the Spirit; for the written code kills, but the Spirit gives life. (II Cor. 3.1-6; RSV).

The situation which concerned Paul in his letters to the church at Corinth, of which this passage is in a sense the epitome, was in two respects similar to our own.

In the first place it was Paul's very success as the first ecumenical evangelist, as the apostle to the nations, which aroused the opposition which he had to face. The fact that he had 'betrothed' the Corinthian church to Christ gave him a special responsibility to present her 'as a pure bride to her one husband' (II Cor. 11.2) and to guard her against false teachers who preach another Jesus. Because of this he became the disciplinarian and conscience of his new converts, arousing the resentment of those who imagined that they were already filled with perfection (I Cor. 4) and who misused the freedom they had by grace. At the same time the freedom and unity in Christ, which he had brought to the Gentiles and Jews alike, aroused the opposition of the stricter adherents of the law, the confessionalists of that day: once the Gentiles had been converted—a good first step for which Paul might be a useful instrument—should they not then be circumcised and brought into the full discipline of the Hebrew-Christian community? It was the sufficiency of Paul and of his Gospel for the permanent life of the Church which his detractors were calling in question.

Second, Paul had constantly to wrestle with the temptation to commend himself as authority, in order to help the Church to grow in grace. Indeed, having been directly attacked he could not avoid this 'boasting' as he called it. He could not help showing that his credentials as a Jew and as a servant of Christ were as good as those of his competitors in terms of the outward acts by which they were demonstrated (II Cor. 11). To have failed to claim his fatherhood in Christ toward the Corinthians would have been an abdication of his responsibility toward them. To have renounced his position of authority, the fruit of his success as an evangelist, would have been unfaithful to his calling. The problem for Paul was to place this personal authority in its proper perspective, to recognize that when he boasted this way he was on the same level with all other men including his opponents, engaging in foolishness, speaking 'like a madman' (11.23), that is, without understanding of the true position of man before God. His struggle with himself in relation to the church at Corinth, of which both letters are full, is to place his own sufficiency, in the very assertion of it, along with the life of the church, before a common judge from whom the power of true life comes. 'Thanks be to God who continually leads us about, captives in Christ's triumphal procession, and everywhere uses us to reveal and spread abroad the fragrance of the knowledge of himself' (II Cor. 2.14, NEB).

This is done, in our passage, in three steps:

1. *Who is sufficient for these things?* (II Cor. 2.16b). This question follows the statement that the Christian is the aroma of Christ, on the reception of which hangs life and death. The answer given a few sentences later is: none of us. The word which we have rendered 'sufficient' following the Authorized (King James) Version and its revisions here, has various meanings in the New Testament. It means 'worthy' in the sense of having an inner personal value. 'Lord,' says the

Roman centurion to Jesus, 'I am not worthy that you should come under my roof' (Matt. 8.8). It means capable or competent, whether by character or training. II Timothy speaks of 'faithful men who will be competent to teach others' (2.2). It may mean simply a sufficient number, or a lot. But the general sense of the word is clear in all its contexts. Whether the perspective is that of the politician who counts votes, the manufacturer who measures technical ability, or the moralist who measures character, what is meant is human capacity for accomplishing human ends, which Paul has transmuted into a question about human capacity to accomplish the ends of God.

It therefore did not surprise or disillusion Paul as much as it has modern Christian or quasi-Christian idealists, that his own message was not more effective, or that the church was so corrupt. The root of this corruption and ineffectiveness is precisely the pride of sufficiency which seizes the successful. It is when the responsible use of human capacity on any level becomes dependence on it to accomplish God's saving purposes that human beings become so thoroughly incapable, even of establishing human community. 'Not that we are sufficient of ourselves, to claim (or count on) anything as coming from us'.

2. *But our sufficiency is of God, who has made us capable.* The same word appears twice, as noun and adjective in the Greek. This is for Paul the first, the central truth without which the other can neither be understood nor accepted. This is, first, the charter of our effective existence in this world. Because this is true Paul dared in his weakness and poverty to preach to the Corinthians and to give them fatherly advice. Because it is true the church in Corinth lived despite itself in a new reality which was its first point of reference. 'Test yourselves—do you not realize that Jesus Christ is in you?' (II Cor. 13.5) 'If any man is in Christ, he is a new creation' (5.17). This is the dynamic ontology of the Church as known in faith. Because it was so, Paul could hope for the church in Corinth, and call it to realize the hope. He could tax it and himself with every burden which

the service of human need and the reconciliation of man with God demands.

But this is, second, also the power by which the Church is enabled to face its own insufficiency in all its depth, to be ruthlessly honest with itself, and to submit to the death of things with which it has hitherto identified its life. It was a struggle for Paul to learn to glory in his weakness, as it was a struggle for the Corinthian church to learn humility and chastity. The problem to which this passage points is a peculiarly modern one: by what power are we enabled to face not just our sins— we may be secretly proud of them—but the unworthiness, the incompetence, the failure of ourselves and our churches? Whence comes the acceptance of us as we are which puts an end to our struggle for self-acceptance and gives us freedom to die?

3. *To be ministers of a new covenant, not in a written code but in the Spirit, for the written code kills, but the Spirit gives life.* Ministry of a new covenant, then, becomes the form of existence of a Church which has accepted its own insufficiency and renounced striving for its own success and commendation. 'Ministers' is, however, a word which masks for the modern mind what this fact implies. The Greek word is somewhat milder than the word for 'slave' but is of the same order and is often interchangeable. The 'minister' does not determine the form of his own service. He does not carry out his own projects. If he is a faithful servant he will use all his talents in doing the task on which he is set, but the sufficiency he has from God is not an injection of competence for the fulfilment of his own plans. Rather the timing, the direction, and the success of his work are in the hands of another. It is another who sets the terms and limits of what can be accomplished, who sets and changes the work to be done at his will. Something of this Paul sought to convey in referring to himself as 'ministering' a letter of recommendation written on the hearts of the Corinthians with the Spirit of God. Probably the modern versions of the Bible

have missed the point of this verse in translating it 'deliver'. Paul not only delivered the faith to the Corinthians, he wrote it on their hearts through his continuing relations with them. But he did so as a scribe would write (and many scribes in his time were slaves or servants), according to dictation, what, when and how his master prescribed, so that the relation established was with his master and not only with himself.

It is precisely in this complete subservience that the meaning of this new existence becomes clear as a ministry in the Spirit which gives life. The written code always sets the self over against it; this is why it kills. The standard of effectiveness, of popularity, even of accuracy in prophetic insight, or of church unity, is always a standard of judgment which turns the Christian and his ecclesiastical institution in upon himself and sets him against his neighbour whether in anxiety over his failures or complacency over his successes. The Spirit on the other hand takes man and his institutions up into his own action, giving to them an existence which is not their own and in which they can forget themselves. The central task becomes to discern the Spirit and to adapt the structure of organizations and plans thereto. This determines the way talents are used and ministries defined, the way plans are made and changed, the way organizations of the Church are created or abolished. This is life. The substance of it is the transformation of human relations which takes place when each person and church becomes a letter from Christ to the other and they explore together what the coming of Christ to the world might mean.

Ecumenical Ministry: the Preparation

This brings us back to the ministry of the World Council of Churches. It has arisen out of the most varied impulses, and many different kinds of hopes and fears have attached themselves to it. In the context of the faith we have been describing, however, the World Council is the chief present organizational embodiment of the ecumenical movement, and the ecumenical movement, at least since Dr Visser 't Hooft has been associated with it, is that dynamic in the life of the churches who confess the name of Christ whereby their own insufficiency is most frankly recognized and openly confessed in order that the transforming work of the Spirit in them may be more clearly discerned and their common ministry to the world more faithfully expressed. It is the focal point where the churches are forced to ask as a question of life or death for themselves, what it means to be the Church of Jesus Christ, and to allow themselves to be changed together into this image. In short the World Council of Churches lives by the same ministry, under the same judgment and in the same reality as the church at Corinth and every Christian community from that time to this. It is given to this ecumenical organization however, as to other Christian communities only in times of extreme crisis or the first flush of conversion, to have no other reality than this—no cultural or religious substance or social influence—to fall back on, when it fails in the confidence it should have through Christ toward God. This is why the life, or death, of the World Council is a constant question to its member churches about their own faithfulness, and a means whereby they are called to discover, on the frontier of their ministry to the world, what it means to be the Church.

This is seen first in the history of the ecumenical movement from a date which corresponded roughly with the coming of Visser 't Hooft into the limelight as editor of the *Student World*. There had of course already been an ecumenical history in the great conferences of Edinburgh 1910, Jerusalem, Stockholm and Lausanne. Each of them had been dominated by a joyous optimism about mission, unity, and a Christian world which had brought the churches a certain distance along the ecumenical path. But the ecumenism of the 1930's, as several writers in this book have documented, was dominated more by a new awareness of how deeply the churches need to be renewed if they are to meet the challenge of the increasingly anti-Christian world. Three foci of this awareness are particularly significant.

1. We see it in the changing attitude of the foreign missionary enterprise after Jerusalem in 1928. Jerusalem was a mature late summer flower of nineteenth century missions. In its deliberations the major non-Christian religions were given full appreciation for the measure of their approach to God, and the Christian message was presented as their fulfilment. Even secularism, western society's humanist rival to the faith, was included, as Kathleen Bliss has shown, in this enveloping confidence. The programme by which non-Christian culture was to be included in Christendom and Christianity was to adapt itself to all that is valuable there seemed well-nigh complete. But already in 1928 this confidence had been badly shaken by the Chinese Revolution the year before. The years to follow revealed with ever increasing force that the apparent dialogue with non-Christian religion and culture which the missionary movement had developed was in large part a monologue and not a conversation with the real forces at work there. Indigenization of the Church in non-Christian lands proved in most cases completely inadequate. The missionary enterprise heard, both from rising nationalist movements and from emancipated local Christians, harsher charges of foreign domination, imperialism, bigotry, legalism, social injustice, and indifference to national hopes than ever before. The long slow process began which is still going on, wherein mission and church, forced and pushed by world revolution, are learning at ever deeper levels how to repent for the false foreignness of the missionary enterprise and present together the true foreignness of the Gospel.

2. We see it in the radical change of emphasis which came over ecumenical work in church and society after the Stockholm Conference in 1925. Stockholm was the realization of a generation's dream: the great churches of Christendom

gathered to make their moral influence felt on society, setting forth principles by which it might be guided, healing its breaches (notably those of the first world war), and planning for service to mankind. But already it stood in the shadow of a new and profounder cleavage in society. The Russian Revolution had succeeded eight years before. In almost every European country Christian forces were lined up alongside conservatives, and the socialist parties were anti-Christian. Once again the optimism of the past proved to have been illusion, even a form of ideology whereby comfortable Christians hid from themselves the forces of judgment which were brewing in the world around them. The ecumenical prophets of the 'thirties, who determined the form of Christian social thinking from that day forth, were those who discerned in and behind the social conflict the judgment of God: Nicolas Berdyaev who called the Russian revolution an intra-historical apocalypse which the Church must accept from the hands of God to bear a free witness in Communist society; Paul Tillich who found the Marxist socialist movement pregnant with divine historical meaning and called on Christians in repentance and hope to join it and make it aware of this religious depth it might otherwise miss; Reinhold Niebuhr who knew both by social experience and by faith that a relative justice is only achieved by setting power against power, and who therefore sided as a Christian with the forces of revolution because he had no confidence in the power of moral suasion to move the self-righteous rich.

Because of the influence of such men as these it has become an axiom of the ecumenical movement in social questions that the Church itself is a social institution with interests, along with those of its members, which are likely to be partial and even opposed to justice, so that the work of God's judgment and grace in the common life of society must be sought by an obedience of thought and action which listens to the enemies as well as the friends of Christendom.

3. We see it in the growing ideological conflict of the thirties, its attack on the Christian faith and the Christian response. There had always been a debate between religion and its cultured despisers. A large part of nineteenth century theology was apologetic, an attempt to make Christianity reasonable and convincing in the thought-forms of the day. The Jerusalem Conference's gentlemanly argument with secular humanism was typical of this effort. In almost every case however the secular opponent of the faith was a form of humanism whose content of personal and social ethics conformed largely with that of the conventional Christianity it opposed. The debate was about religion and God, not about man and society. With the coming of Marx-Leninism, however, both Christians and secular humanists were confronted with a power remoulding society which broke the traditional consensus about man, and frankly used thought as an instrument of revolutionary action rather than as a means for investigating and stating truth. In the wake, then, of the Marxist challenge other ideologies arose, each claiming in similar fashion to place thought within the framework of a total framework of meaningful action: nationalist, fascist, nazi, or perhaps some more private world of life-worship, sexual fulfilment or rebellious self-expression.

Christians have responded to this rude rupture of traditional communication, this breach of the peace of the common life, in such various ways that one scarcely dares speak of ecumenical movement here. Some have persisted in failing to recognize an ideology for what it is, and have sought to harmonize Christian truth with each of them. Others have made of the faith itself an ideology, proclaiming the structure of Christendom as the answer to the classless society. In each case however the result has been only to reveal the tragic failure of Christians to take their own Gospel seriously. 'It is against the very essence of our faith,' wrote Visser 't Hooft in the midst of the ideological controversies of the 'thirties, 'to believe in salvation by programmes.'[1] So also, he continued, to present Christianity as truth which is the answer to the questions of man as he is, which man can control and with which he can achieve his own ends, is to deny the truth of Christ who confronts and questions us. The rough challenge of the ideologies has come to mean for the ecumenical movement, as a result of these years of struggle, on the one hand a warning against the ideological elements in the Church itself, and on the other a calling to a life of witness and obedience which alone can demonstrate another reality than that in which the ideologist believes.

Thus the challenge of the world in which the World Council of Churches was born. Had the ecumenical movement only to face these questions to Christian existence, however, its task would have been far lighter and its reality more shallow than it is. All the world's criticisms of the Church are based to some degree on misunderstanding and on the world's own standards and desires. The temper of ecumenism today is the result of having stood in the crossfire of two frontiers at once. For when these defenders of the Church retreated from the worldly battle line to the citadel of theology and the Bible, they found there a far more accurate and devastating attack upon their Christian self-understanding than any which the world had to offer. The ecumenical movement was forged not only in the social events of the 1930's but also in the biblical and theological renewal of which Suzanne de Diétrich writes, whose foremost personality was Karl Barth, but which permeated every nation and confession with its questions and its challenge. It was in the encounter with the Word of God that ecumenism learned that the crisis of human life is far deeper than even the Marxists imagine, indeed that secular revolutionary ideology is but a distorted reflection of what happens to us all in the death and resurrection of Christ. J. L. Hromadka's greatest contribution to the ecumenical movement has been to hold before it continually the depth of this crisis and the hope for the life of the

[1] W. A. Visser 't Hooft, *None Other Gods*, pp. 114ff.

Church which is born in it. It was in Bible study and biblical theology that the churches grasped anew the dynamic reality of their own existence in the covenant of grace as witnesses to the reconciling peace of God. It was here that the struggle for social justice and human freedom took on its true urgency and importance. It was here also that the churches learned that patience in hope, that free witness in love which penetrates totalitarian systems with another reality.

The struggle still continues in the churches over the nature of biblical authority and interpretation, and its relation to tradition and natural reason. It would prejudice the ecumenical dialogue to sponsor one view in this context. But the fact may be recorded that the World Council of Churches has not waited for these questions to be solved. Throughout the twenty-five to thirty years with which we are here concerned, its ideas, policies and actions have been continually made, challenged and remade by regular searching of and engagement with the biblical message. 'Biblical realism,' the term which Hendrik Kraemer coined to describe this approach to missionary work which he proposed at Tambaram in 1938, is a fundamental ecumenical reality.

'Let the Church be the Church'

'The first duty of the Church,' proclaimed the Oxford Conference in 1937, as an answer to this double challenge of the world and the Word of God, 'is to be in very deed the church —confessing the true faith, committed to the fulfilment of the will of Christ its only lord, and united to him in a fellowship of love and service.'

It was not ecclesiastical reaction but rediscovery of the work of Christ in the world which moved the Oxford fathers to so emphasize the being of the Church and to give it just this vocation. 'We do not call the world to be like ourselves,' the message continues, 'for we are already too like the world. Only as we ourselves repent, both as individuals and as corporate bodies, can the Church call men to repentance. The call to ourselves and to the world is to Christ.' From that time until today the ecumenical movement, guided by the profound conviction of Visser 't Hooft himself, has never been allowed to forget that through the devastating force of world events and the searching questions of the Bible, God is carrying on 'a profoundly serious conversation' with the churches about what it means to be the Church.[1] The subsequent history of ecumenism might well be described as the story of the Church's rediscovery of the form of its being on the frontiers where its existence is challenged.

What then is this form of the Church, and how has it been discovered in the World Council's ministry? No exhaustive list can be given for this discovery, and renewal takes place in every ecumenical meeting where Christians are torn out of old contexts and confronted with new realities, biblical, churchly, and secular. But the following, reflected as they are in the essays of this volume, may illustrate both the process and the questions it raises for the years to come.

1. *Ecumenical work in the field of Church and society.* This ranges from the experience of the German Confessing Church, which Martin Fischer describes, to the present and future problems with which Paul Abrecht deals. Dietrich Bonhoeffer in 1935 was one of the first to challenge the ecumenical movement in these terms by putting to it the question implied in the very existence of the Confessing Church in Germany. This church had come into existence by the act of confessing its faith at the Synod of Barmen over against the political and religious powers of Nazi Germany and by this confession, at once political and theological, it lived. 'Because the Confessing Church has learned in its struggle that its confession alone must

[1] W. A. Visser 't Hooft, *The Wretchedness and the Greatness of the Church* (1944), pp. 33ff.

determine the whole life of the Church from the preaching of the Gospel to the management of finances, because there is no neutral unconfessing space in it, it puts to every partner in dialogue immediately the question of confession.' Does the ecumenical movement, asked Bonhoeffer, claim in any sense to express the Church? If so it too must face the question where and in what way it is called upon to confess the faith, to put its existence at stake in its proclamation of the Gospel and in the action of its obedience.[1]

It is far more difficult for the World Council of Churches in the complex post-war world than for the Confessing Church confronting Nazism to discover the concrete form of its confession of Christ in society. The way of setting forth 'long-range goals, standards and principles,' which still characterized the social thinking of the Oxford Conference to a large degree, is far easier. Nevertheless Bonhoeffer's challenge describes the heart of what ecumenical work in church and society in the post-war world is trying to do, as Paul Abrecht describes it in this volume. This work involves a far more complex analysis— which must be at once theological and social-scientific—of modern society than was necessary when the world was dominated by one or another ideology which determined the basic pattern of the common life. In this analysis theology and the social sciences are always in danger of losing contact with one another, as indeed are the social sciences among themselves. The further from decision and action these analyses wander the greater discord becomes. But the standpoint of the Church which analyzes, as the World Council of Churches expresses it, is itself that of continual action in Christian obedience on the various frontiers the world affords. A pronouncement in council is only one form by which the ecumenical movement confesses Christ in society. Behind it lies the continuing process whereby Christians from all walks of life meet and question one

[1] "Die Bekennende Kirche und die Ökumene" in *Gesammelte Schriften* vol. i; pp. 240ff.

another about their Christian obedience seeking, and being corrected by, the mind of Christ as the Church discovers it in this process together.

It is a humbling and often unsuccessful process. But through it we learn, in a new way, something about the relation between the Holy Spirit and our prayers and perplexity. 'We know not,' says Rom. 8.26, 'what we should pray for as we ought but the Spirit itself maketh intercession for us with groanings which cannot be uttered'. Nothing more aptly describes the spirit in which our prayers and our acts take place in this present world. We agonize, we act in fear and trembling as well as in love. We do not know what we ought to do in situations like the race conflict in South Africa or the balance of terror, due to atomic weapons, in which the world is caught. Yet this agony, this fear and trembling is itself a witness to the work and action of the Spirit. It is far more convincing than any pronouncements of high ideals which cannot be applied could be. A report which a group of Christian scientists, politicians and military men produced under the auspices of the Study Division of the World Council in 1958 on *Christians and the Prevention of War in an Atomic Age* is a typical example. It gives no Christian solution to the problem, yet it shows in its very uncertainty, in the depths of the seriousness with which it takes the problem, and man's attempt to wrestle with it, a relation to the work of the Holy Spirit which is the profoundest witness which we can bear these days to our Lord. 'The Spirit also', says the same verse, 'helpeth our infirmities . . . and he that searcheth the hearts knoweth what is in the mind of the Spirit because he maketh intercession for the saints according to the will of God'. We have learnt anew what this intercession of Christ on our behalf means and how it sustains not only us but the whole world.

In short we have learned that the whole business of Christian social action is a matter of service, of ministry, which shares the ministry of Christ, of witness to Christ in a changing situation.